D1832967

IMPERIAL RULE IN INDIA

IMPERIAL RULE IN INDIA

BEING AN EXAMINATION OF THE PRINCIPLES
PROPER TO THE GOVERNMENT
OF DEPENDENCIES

THEODORE MORISON

GYAN

Published by

Gyan Publishing House
5, Ansari Road
Daryaganj, New Delhi-110002
Phone: 011-47034999, 9811692060
E-mail: books@gyanbooks.com

Distribution Network
gyanbooks.com
India, USA, Canada, UK, Australia, France

© Publisher
All rights reserved. No part of this work may be reproduced, stored, adapted, or transmitted in any form or by any means, electronic, mechanical, photocopying, micro-filming, recording or otherwise, or translated in any language, without the prior written permission of the copyright owner and the publisher.

ISBN: 978-81-212-8834-7 (PB)
First Published, 1899

2nd Impression 2023

Printed at: Gyan Press, Delhi.

The book is sold subject to the condition that it shall not, by way of trade or otherwise, be lent, resold, hired out, or otherwise circulated without the prior publisher's written consent.

Imperial Rule In India
Author: Theodore Morison

IMPERIAL RULE IN INDIA

IMPERIAL RULE IN INDIA

BEING AN EXAMINATION OF THE PRINCIPLES
PROPER TO THE GOVERNMENT
OF DEPENDENCIES

BY

THEODORE MORISON

WESTMINSTER
ARCHIBALD CONSTABLE & Co.
2 WHITEHALL GARDENS.
1899

TO MY WIFE

PREFACE

ALTHOUGH an author cannot pretend to dictate what use shall be made of the ideas he puts forward, I should like at the outset to state explicitly that my intention has not been to furnish reactionaries with another argument against free institutions.

Those who believe that popular government is the highest form of political organization to which mankind has yet attained, may still be compelled to recognise that certain peoples are not yet capable of managing their own affairs. Admirers of representative institutions have hitherto chiefly concerned themselves with fully developed nationalities, and have not been to the trouble of explaining how less perfectly homogeneous peoples are to fit themselves for that form of government.

This book is intended to suggest how the transition from one phase of political development to another may be effected; and from a passing reference to the subject in his "Liberty", I gather that the solution I have proposed would not have been repugnant to Mill himself. For people in this early stage of development there is, he says, nothing but implicit obedience to an Akbar or a Charlemagne if they are so fortunate as to find one.

M. A.-O. College,
Aligarh,
N. W. P.

CONTENTS

CHAP.		PAGE
I	THE FIRST POSTULATE OF INDIAN INDEPENDENCE	1
II	PSEUDO-LIBERALISM IN INDIA	12
III	ON THE FORMATION OF NATIONALITIES	32
IV	THE EMPRESS OF INDIA	42
V	REGARDING SOME MAXIMS OF POPULAR GOVERNMENT	55
VI	PUBLIC OPINION IN INDIA	68
VII	THE COLLECTOR	86
VIII	THE PRESS IN INDIA	96
IX	EDUCATION	113
X	THE PART OF THE EMPRESS IN THE ADMINISTRATION OF INDIA	133

CHAPTER I

THE FIRST POSTULATE OF INDIAN INDEPENDENCE

IN the background of every Englishman's mind is probably to be found the conviction that it is our duty so to govern India that she may one day be able to govern herself, and as an autonomous unit take her place in the great confederation of the British Empire. This is the ultimate justification of our Asiatic dominion, and a statesman who ventured to advocate the alternative policy that India should be kept in a state of perpetual vassalage, as the milch cow of England, would be hooted from public life.

No doubt the benevolent intentions of the British electorate are vaguely conceived and liable to considerable modification in the future; no reasonable man supposes that the time for executing them has come, or is likely soon to come, within the range of practical politics; but once convinced of the ultimate objective of their policy, I maintain that it is the duty of the English people in whose hands lie the destinies of India, to examine, from time to time, the general tendency of their administrative measures, and to consider whether the policy which their agents in the East are pursuing, is preparing the way for the eventual emancipation of India. The test of a truly liberal policy should be that it tends eventually, and in the long run, to put the people of India in a position to manage their own affairs.

I do not believe that the people of India are at present capable of erecting a government of their own, nor do I think that if the present policy is continued they are on the way to become so; and yet I recognise that the martial races of India are brave and make excellent soldiers, that the native civilians are possessed of great intelligence and that they have proved on the Bench of every High Court in India that they are capable of discharging the highest judicial functions. The general level of education is no doubt much lower than in France or England, but in order to bring the autonomy of India within the range of practical politics the standard of civilization required is not that of France or England, but rather of Bulgaria or Mexico; and India is not so far behind either of these nations that upon these grounds her emancipation can be indefinitely postponed.

But India is wanting in the one qualification essential to independence, inasmuch as she possesses no sentiment of nationality. Where this sentiment exists it is possible that a people in a comparatively low state of civilization may maintain an independent existence, but where it is absent neither bravery, intelligence nor civilization avails to keep off anarchy, which would lay the people at the feet of the first invader.

That India is neither a nation like France, nor a collection of nations like Europe, hardly needs demonstration. If the strong hand of England were withdrawn, the different races and creeds which are scattered up and down her towns and villages would never agree to a common line of action. It is just conceivable that they might unite to throw off the English yoke, but they would not consent for long to subordinate their racial and religious jealousies to the common good; they might under great provocation form a strong opposition; they never could frame an administration. It is true that there are sentiments which possibly contain the germs of nationality: the Muhamadans, the Sikhs, the Parsis and some Hindu castes are knit together by ties which resemble in some ways the ties of nationality; but the Muhamadans, the Sikhs and others are not congregated in definite localities, but are dispersed about the country, unassimilated fragments in a heterogeneous conglomerate. Hence it comes that in India such national sentiments as do exist are not associated with any territorial limits; there is no division of the Indian soil which the Muhamadan or Parsi can call his own or in which he can claim an interest, to which another people has not as good a right.

The Muhamadans are in some ways the most definite and homogeneous political unit in India; they are heirs of a common civilization and common traditions of glory, and they are conscious to an extent unsurpassed in India of their corporate existence. If the 57 million Muhamadans of India were all collected in one province or tract of country, if for instance, the north of India from Peshawar to Agra were inhabited exclusively by Muhamadans, a national spirit associated with those territorial limits would already be in process of formation, which would suggest a partial solution of the present problem. But the Muhamadans are, as a matter of fact, scattered in isolated groups all over the peninsula, and in consequence such sentiment of nationality as they do possess, links them not with Sikhs and Bengalis, with whom they share the soil, but with their coreligionists wherever they are found, be it in Arabia or Persia or within the frontiers of India. So little do the Muhamadans regard India as their own country that their great poet, Hali, has compared his people to guests who have outstayed their welcome, and lamented that they ever left their native homes for India:

"Morning and evening our eyes now behold that which we thought would be the end of thy gracious reception.

"Quickly hast thou broken all thy promises and

pledges; O India, we were told aright that thou wast faithless.

"From every side we hear thee say that the guest is unwelcome who tarries long."

* * *

"Hast thou ever beheld the men of Islam in this plight before? Was this the Islam which we brought with us from Arabia?

"Oh Mill of revolving Time, thou hast ground us small; enough; have done; what boots it thee to grind us further?"

* * *

"As the host of the Greeks turned back from thy border (India), would that in like manner we had turned back baffled from thy door."

(*Shikwah Hind V.* M. Altaf Hosain Hali.)

The views held by the Muhamadans (certainly the most aggressive and truculent of the peoples of India) are alone sufficient to prevent the establishment of an independent Indian Government. Were the Afghan to descend from the north upon an autonomous India, the Muhamadans, instead of uniting with the Sikhs and Hindus to repel him, would be drawn by all the ties of kinship and religion to join his flag.

The sentiment of nationality in which India is wanting is likely to be of greater importance in the future than it has ever been in the past. The present development of the world seems to be in the direction of states which are firmly knit together by the bonds of nationality, and India may find herself surrounded by powers which are more compact and homogeneous than herself by reason of the possession of this sentiment. In a struggle with these states India, loosely and imperfectly united, would inevitably succumb. The development of a national sentiment is an example of the "integration of the organism" which is the result of the struggle for survival; in an earlier stage of development states were able to do without it, because they were brought in contact only with states as imperfectly homogeneous as themselves, but in the future those states, which are also nations, will in the struggle for existence destroy and absorb those which are not permeated with this invigorating sentiment.

If then India is ever to govern herself, it can only be on condition of developing a sense of national unity, and the disinterested beneficence of our rule may be tested by considering whether any such sentiment is being produced in India.

Although the truth is hidden from our eyes by the very stability of British rule, by the Pax Britannica of political posters, India has made no progress in this direction at all. It is commonly believed by the people themselves that the hostility of the Hindus and Muhamadans is increasing and that the chances of their amalgamating into one nationality are diminishing. This hostility is certainly most marked in the classes which are characteristic products of English rule, and, contrariwise, riots between the two communities are rarest in those parts of India which are officially described as the most backward. These quarrels are almost unknown in Rajputana and Central India, and even in British territory Hindu and Muhamadan landowners, whose existence is mostly spent in sleepy country villages, live side by side on terms of respectful and somewhat distant friendship. It is the lawyers and the schoolmasters of big towns who organise the agitations and chicanery by which strife is bred between the two communities. I have very often asked natives of India what in their opinion was the cause of this growing ill-will between Hindus and Muhamadans, and the answer I have generally received is that it is due to English education. This is somewhat inconsequential, but it calls attention to the salient fact that the antipathy between the two peoples has followed in the train of English ideas. The fact is generally acknowledged, and I do not think the cause is far to seek. We have never aimed at the creation of a national sentiment in India, and with the best intentions have founded institutions which have a disintegrating tendency. The next chapter will show how the progress of India has been arrested by prematurely introducing the principles of popular government.

It would, however, be inconsiderate to close this chapter without some reference to those politicians who contend that India is a nation and that they are her chosen representatives. The Indian National Congress is a political organization which held its 14th annual meeting during the Christmas holidays of 1898. These politicians have seen that the natives of India have some interests in common as against their English conquerors. The obvious fact that our dominion is founded on the supremacy of the English race has no doubt created a broad and simple line of division between the English and the natives of the soil; but these politicians forget that the combination of independent factions against the government may make a strong opposition, but will not form a united party. In its earlier years the Congress achieved very considerable success; it obtained a great deal of notoriety, and many of the people of India watched its success with secret satisfaction even if they did not sympathise with the political programme to which it was pledged, because they were naturally pleased to see the natives of the soil making head against the English. Mr. Bradlaugh was responsible for a phrase to the effect that the Congress was the anvil upon which an Indian nationality was being hammered into being, and the promoters of the movement took to calling themselves and the natives of the soil, "Indians". * The success of the National Congress did certainly indicate, in a very ominous way, that the dissatisfaction caused by our reserving all substantial political privileges to ourselves was widespread, and that the people were willing to sympathise with any movement which aimed at curtailing our monopoly. Like all Oppositions composed of mutually hostile groups, the Congress came to grief in framing a programme. The Congress is deeply pledged to the introduction of representative institutions into India. As soon as this was realised the entire Muhamadan community, being to the Hindus in a minority of one to four, declared against the movement. Latterly other hostilities have broken out, which prove that even the loose union necessary for an Opposition is not yet possible among the different sections of Indian society; orthodox Hindus of the old school have been offended at the pretensions of the Congress politicians to represent Hindu society, seeing that their manners and methods of political agitation are flagrantly foreign to Indian ideas. The consequence is that the movement now only represents a clique in which the general public is losing all

* This is a term which I should be very loth to apply to the natives of India, because the usage of the English language has made the word Indian (when used as a substantive) synonymous with savage.

interest; even in Bengal, the country of its origin, the Congress seems to be held in scant esteem. The Bangovasi, the most influential vernacular paper in Bengal, said on June 18th, 1898:

"With Englishmen political agitation is a sacred duty.... but what is our political agitation like? It is, we feel ashamed to say, an annual merry-making extending over 3 days, a periodical gathering of English educated Babus, bent on enjoying a holiday. In three days in the year they make themselves merry, deliver cut and dried speeches, pass foolish resolutions, and gather materials for equally foolish writing for a whole year and then depart home and then——what then? All this ranting and blustering and speech-making, all this waste of money ends as it must, like a dream, in nothingness."

But the reader must not suppose that these politicians do not take their labours seriously. In justice to the Congress I will close with an extract from one of its most ardent supporters:

"It was feared, even a couple of days before the meeting of the Congress, that many leaders, owing to the plague and divers other causes, would not be able to attend the present session. Almost all, however, were there at the right moment. One prominent Congressman, before leaving for Amraoti, wrote to Mr. Mudholkar, Secretary to the Reception Committee, to the following effect: 'I come more dead than alive, as I am suffering dreadfully from a bad pain all over my body. Remain prepared to read the burial service over my grave.' The delegate kept his word, though ill, and to the relief of Mr. Mudholkar, he had not to read the burial service over his grave. Babu Boikantha Nath Sen of Berhampur was actually suffering from fever and a bad cold, and his wife seriously ailing when he started for Amraoti. Babu Ambica Charan Mozamdar of Faridpur, who had come to Calcutta with the object of proceeding to Berar, received an urgent telegram to the effect that his wife had been dangerously ill: he returned to Faridpur, made some arrangements for the treatment of his wife, and then ran for Amraoti, leaving her to the care of God, for the purpose of serving his country. Babu Bhupendra Nath Bose had an attack of diarrhœa and severe toothache, and yet started with the other delegates amidst the earnest protests of his near and dear ones. Some of the Bombay and Poona delegates as they had been in quarantine, had to spend a number of days in the Segregation Camp. Mr. W. C. Bonerjee himself was also detained while coming direct from England to Amraoti, as he had to pass through Bombay: he was, however, released after a detention of six hours. There is yet hope for India when our leaders are prepared to make these sacrifices for the welfare of their dear, though ill-fated country."

CHAPTER II

PSEUDO-LIBERALISM IN INDIA

OUR dominion in India is contemporaneous with the triumphant progress of Democracy over Europe, and since the English electors have acquired the ultimate control of our Indian policy they have consistently pressed the Government of India to adopt a policy in harmony with their own sympathies. We have found it impossible to give India a completely democratic constitution, but we have given her what are usually considered the attributes of a free government. I believe that the modern tendency towards further disintegration has been caused by these free institutions. The principal of them are: a free press, the right of public association and debate, trial by jury, and the tentative introduction of the principle of representation on the provincial councils and municipalities.

The inevitable result of free institutions is to encourage the growth of parties, and in a country in which there is no sentiment of national unity, parties will be formed along the lines of cleavage already existing. In India the lines of cleavage are principally those of race and religion, and it is upon these lines that parties are nowadays forming themselves; the result is to accentuate those very antipathies and jealousies which prevent India from becoming a nation. The division between the Hindus and Muhamadans represents the deepest line of cleavage in the Indian people, and consequently the two principal parties of contemporary Indian politics are the Hindu and the Muhamadan; and the disputes on what are called political questions are in reality but phases of a religious feud which is always on the verge of becoming civil war. English politicians, who cannot realize that there may be countries in which there is no sentiment of nationality, are apt to fancy that they recognize in the dissensions of the Hindus and the Muhamadans only the harmless rivalry of parties with which they are familiar at home. As a matter of fact the movements which have received real popular support in recent years have not been merely manifestations of a healthy interest in public affairs, but rather the outcome of deep-seated hatreds which have before now deluged the country with blood, and which would do so again were it not for the fear of British bayonets. I will first attempt to show the true character of the contest between the Hindus and the Muhamadans, in order to prove that these are dissensions which make for the destruction of an Indian nationality, and which it is therefore our duty to stifle; in the second place I shall point out that popular institutions stimulate these ancient feuds, for conducting which they provide scope, and that existing animosities are envenomed by mutual recriminations on the platform and in the press.

The most important popular movement of recent years was undoubtedly the agitation organised by the Hindus against the slaughter of kine which they consider sacred. A society, with branches in different parts of India, was formed for the Protection of the Cow. Lecturers were appointed who travelled from town to town and village to village; pamphlets and leaflets called "The Cry of the Cow" etc. were distributed broadcast, and public meetings were held which were reported in the newspapers. A Rajah told me that he also received private letters urging him to further the agitation, in the postscript of which was added that if he left this duty undischarged it would be considered as heinous "as the murder of 500 cows." The result of the movement was to excite the hostility of the Hindus against the two beef-eating peoples of India, the English and the Muhamadans. The object of some at least of the agitators was to provoke ill-will against the English; I was told by an English Commissioner who had seen a copy, that a coloured plate was circulated among the people, in which the Hindu Gods were represented punishing a red-faced monkey for maltreating the cow. The monkey is an ill-famed beast in India and the equivalent of a term of abuse, and the rubicund countenance ascribed to him is an obvious allusion to English complexions. But the peace of the country was more seriously disturbed by the strife which this movement bred between the Hindus and the Muhamadans. The Muhamadans were enraged at the attempt to deprive them arbitrarily of their supplies of beef which, being cheap and in small demand, constitutes almost the only meat consumed by the poorer classes of Muhamadans. They accordingly retaliated by slaughtering an increased number of cows, sometimes in the prescribed slaughter-houses, and sometimes, when zeal outran discretion, in such a conspicuous manner as was best calculated to outrage Hindu sentiment. Some Muhamadan divines began to favour the opinion that the sacrifice of cows was peculiarly grateful to the Deity, and there was a tendency to substitute them for goats and sheep which had hitherto been found sufficient to appease his wrath. It is not surprising that this agitation was followed by what were known as Cow-killing Riots, in which blood was freely shed; in many cases the police were unable to cope with the infuriated mobs, and the military had to be called out. Had the movement been allowed to reach its natural conclusion, it would have rekindled the fire which set all India ablaze in the days of Aurangzeb. And this agitation, with its disastrous consequences, owed its success to the use of free institutions. The press, the platform, the distribution of polemical literature, in fact the whole paraphernalia of a political campaign were employed to spread dissensions between peoples who must live in amity if India is to become a nation.

In March 1898 another controversy in the papers showed that the Hindus and the Muhamadans are not divided upon political principles properly so called, but solely by religious or racial animosity. The Hindus of the North West Provinces approached the Lieutenant-Governor with a petition that the court records should be kept in Hindi (their national alphabet) instead of the Persian or Muhamadan character, as had hitherto been the case; this was fiercely resented by the Muhamadans, who saw in it an attempt to disqualify them for one branch of the public service; the question in debate involved no political principle at all, but it excited men's passions because it was an incident in the struggle in which one community attempts to overreach or discredit the other.

There is indeed one question of political principle upon which the Hindus and the Muhamadans have taken opposite sides, and that is the question of representative institutions, but this too is only an instructive example of the way in which party principles are formed in India. The Muhamadans oppose the introduction of the principle of representation because they are in the minority and are well aware that the elections would always be contested on racial and religious lines, and that therefore Muhamadans would always be defeated at the poll.

When such is the rancour of racial ill-will, is it wise on our part to allow the two communities to form themselves into parties and to give them free scope to attack and vilify each other? If continental critics were aware of the extent to which we have introduced free institutions in India, they would say that we have acted on the cynical motto "Divide et impera"; for these free institutions have fomented the dissensions among the conquered people and diminished the likelihood of their uniting against us. Indeed natives of India who are aware of the growth of ill-will between the Hindus and Muhamadans of recent years, have often said that these quarrels have been promoted by us for our own ends. The Jami Ul Ulum said on the 21st March, 1897: "For some time past the Government has been secretly pursuing the policy 'Divide and Rule' by showing favour to the Hindus and Muhamadans alternately." As that accusation stands, it is not true; the district officers do their best to patch up the quarrels of the two peoples, and an officer would be thought badly of by his superiors who allowed such animosites to reach an acute stage; but though our collectors have attempted to check the feeling in detail, the general tendency of our policy in recent years has embittered the relations of Hindus and Muhamadans.

To deal first of all with the press:—a generation which can remember how often the nations of Europe have been goaded to the verge of war by irresponsible journalists, will not need many illustrations to be convinced of the harm which a free press can do in India. The nations of Europe, however, enjoy some natural safeguards against the evils of journalism; they speak different languages and therefore one people is not compelled to hear all the evil spoken of it by another; they inhabit separate quarters of the earth and are not chafed by daily contact with irritating national characteristics. But Hindus and Muhamadans inhabit the same towns and the same street; the Hindu is infuriated by seeing the Muhamadan purchase his beefsteak for dinner; the Muhamadan is disturbed in his prayers to the one God by the sound of heathenish music accompanying a Hindu idol down the street. To these national grounds of dislike are added purely personal animosities. The Brahmin remembers how Muhamad Khan had him beaten with a scavenger's broom, and the Muhamadan bears a grudge against that "dog of a Kaffir", Kishan Chand, who cheated him over the mortgage. The Muhamadan takes up a newspaper conducted by Hindus, and finds his own people bespattered with abuse, and the Hindu robber, who treacherously murdered a Muhamadan general, extolled as a national hero; he goes round with the article in his pocket to a Muhamadan editor and helps him to compose a coarse attack upon the chastity of Hindu women. Here is the chronicle of a typical little affair between the communities, as reported in their papers:—

The Hindu "Hitavadi" leads off on April 30th, 1897, as follows:

"Out of spite against some Hindu milkman who had refused to supply him with milk for a feast, Syed Ali Ullah, a respectable Mussalman gentleman of Kushtia, killed 25 cows near a public road."

Next week (May 8th, 1897,) the Muhamadan "Mihir O Sudhakkar" retorts:

"The garden in which the cows were slaughtered is enclosed on all sides, but still the slaughter offended the Hindu who oppressed and annoyed the Mussalmans in various ways. Many of the invited Mussalmans were prevented from going to the feast or taking part in its management.... on April 25th, an attempt was made by the Hindus to set fire to the Syed's house, and the attempt has not yet been given up. The Hindu students of the local school refuse to sit with the Mussalman students. Syed Ali Ullah's bearers, washermen, barbers, have struck work: the Hindu pleaders of the local bar have resolved not to take his cases at fees less than 10 Rs."

This is followed by a scandalous attack upon Hindu women, which is reproduced (for the better irritation of the public) in the Hindu "Hitavadi" on May 14th, as follows:

"There are few widows in Hindu households who have not had 2, 3, 4, 5, foetuses destroyed: it is clearly proved by the case instituted by Sandamini, at Benares, that Hindu widows do not incur social blame by committing adultery; there is slight trouble only if foetuses cannot be destroyed."

Next week (May 22nd, 1897,) another Hindu paper, the "Bangovasi," joins the fray to say: "In this hot country, beef-eating cannot suit the Mussalmans: they eat beef out of spite against the Hindus."

The irritation between the two communities was apparently dying down in Bareilly in 1898, but the newspapers tried to fan it into flame again. The "Vedic Dharma" (quoted by the Muhamadan "Rohilkand Gazette" on 8th March, 1898) warned the Hindus against cultivating friendship and affection towards the Mussalmans, who are their "enemies, oppressors, and murderers."

A month later a Muhamadan paper follows in the same strain:

"Hindus are very enthusiastic in other matters also. They beat down Mussalmans even in race feeling. Just think how all the 'pot-bellied' ones (*i.e.* Hindus) were stirred up in connection with Mr. Tilak's case and, raising the cry of 'Sympathy! Sympathy'! collected thousands of rupees for the defence of 'an enemy of the country' like him. The writer has heard of the recent reconciliation and concord between the Hindus and Muhamadans at Bareilly. But it is all bosh. A libel suit was instituted against the Mussalman editor of the 'Rohilkand Gazette', and several Hindus gave evidence against him. Is this what is meant by concord between the two communities in that town? The continuance of a tension of feeling between them would on such an occasion have been much better than the so-called amity. In the former case some Muhamadans would have, from race feeling, espoused the cause of the poor Muhamadan editor against the (prosecuting) Hindu. The fact of the matter is that those Mussalmans who seek concord with the Hindus, are downright fools. Hindus will never be faithful, however much friendship you may cultivate with them." (Mashir-i-Sultanat, 3rd May, 1898.)

Rich as is the vocabulary of parliamentary invective in Europe nowadays, it is not yet customary for one party to accuse the ladies of the other of unchastity, a charge which is often bandied between Hindus and Muhamadans. Indeed the characteristic difference between the political scurrilities of Europe and India is this,—that Hindu or Muhamadan politicians do not confine themselves to abusing individual popular leaders (in which case they could probably find in Europe a precedent for the most offensive accusations), but scatter their aspersions over a whole community, a sufficient indication that they are moved by racial and not by political feeling.

Another very obvious line of cleavage in India is the division between Englishmen and natives of the country, and wherever popular institutions give the opportunity, these two have been constituted into opposite factions. Each section of the people is continually wounding the other's feelings in the press, not by difference of opinion, but by offensive reflections upon the national characteristics of the other. I am inclined to think that the English newspapers are the worst offenders in this case, for they often betray the insolent contempt of conquerors without being aware of it. Written principally for the Anglo-Indian community, they give vent to feelings which it is useless to hope can ever be wholly overcome, but which ought never to be publicly expressed, and which are reproduced and commented on in the vernacular press. It can never serve any good purpose to contrast one people's virtues with another's shortcomings; and one evil consequence may be seen in the discussion which occupies considerable space in native newspapers upon the comparative chastity of English and native women; these discussions which inflict wounds that can never be forgiven, constitute a tremendous indictment against the liberty of the press in India.

I will take but one case which occurred only a year ago, and in which the spark that set the whole native press in a blaze of anger was dropped, accidentally I believe, by an Englishman. Sir E. Collen is reported to have said in the discussion on the Cantonments Act Amendment Bill, that

"India was a land where prostitution is not regarded otherwise than as an ordinary condition of life, and where the profession of a prostitute is not looked upon as one of unqualified shame." What Sir E. Collen meant by these words I have no special means of knowing, but it is obvious that they can bear a meaning which is no slur upon the women of India, and it was in that sense that I understood them when I first saw the report of his speech. In the native press, however, (both English and vernacular,) a tempest of indignation was let loose. I cannot here attempt to reproduce the many articles written on this subject; I must ask the reader to accept the following extract as typical of what he would have seen in almost any vernacular paper:

"It is probable that Sir E. Collen while he was uttering the fearful libel against Indian women was with closed eyes seeing visions of the London divorce courts and of some convivial gatherings in England. The chastity and purity of Indian women and the veneration in which religion is held in India are things which cannot enter into the conception of a man like the Hon. Military Member.

* * *

"In England the injured husband sues his faithless wife and her paramour in a law-court and parts with his conjugal love for money.

* * *

"In England a woman whose adultery has been

proved in a law-court finds lots of men eager for her hand, as if the highest conjugal happiness is attained by marrying an adulteress. It is the height of insolence for a people accustomed to such sights to call in question the purity of Indian women." (Basumati, July 29th, 1897.)

Next to the free press, representative institutions have most tended to envenom existing jealousies. The principle of popular election has been partially introduced into the Municipal and District Boards, two-thirds of the Commissioners being elected by the rate-payers and one-third nominated. Could any reasonable man expect the communities which are at daily and hourly strife with each other to sink their ill-will at the time of the elections and contest the elections upon political principles? The majority of the rate-payers of Calcutta are Hindus, and accordingly, in the Annual Statement exhibiting the "Moral and Material Progress and Condition of India," 1896—97, we find in the report upon the Calcutta Municipality the following:

"The general body of the 75 Commissioners had gradually deprived the executive of power and devoted itself to debating rather than to acting, and the Commissioners are perhaps too much dominated by a clique in which Trade interests, the Moslem community and the European inhabitants are practically unrepresented" (p. 5). In the interior of Bengal we find that in 27 municipalities "the Government in consequence of the backwardness of the locality or *of the intensity of party feeling* exercises the power of nomination." (p. 6.) In Europe the intensity of party feeling denotes a healthy interest in public affairs; in India it paralyses self-government; the report should have said *race feeling* not party feeling. It is needless to multiply instances: wherever the population is divided between the two communities in proportions sufficient to make a fight, the municipal elections are conducted upon the lines of racial or religious hostility and the ill-will between the two is exasperated. I was present in 1896, at a representative gathering of Muhamadans from all parts of Upper India, and we had an informal discussion upon politics. The grievance of which almost all complained and for which they were seeking a remedy was the oppression they suffered at the hands of the Hindus on the Municipalities; the only exceptions were from those towns in which the Government has secured the representation of the Muhamadan minority by law.

The untoward results of free institutions in India are best illustrated by the history of the National Congress. That body is an advocate of representative institutions, and by the operation of its own principles has notably added to the bitterness of racial antipathies. India, say these politicians, is ripe for popular Government, and the National Congress plays the part of a constitutional Opposition. If this position is conceded it cannot be denied that one of the legitimate functions of an Opposition is to criticise and even to discredit the Government, with a view sooner or later to taking its place. Now the present Government of India consists principally of Englishmen, and I cannot see that the Congress is illogical in attempting to discredit, firstly, the Government, and in the second place, Englishmen in India generally; it is the recognised way of imparting to the world the charge that all Oppositions bring, viz., that the present ministry has not the confidence of the country, that it has grossly mismanaged public affairs and that the statesmen of the Opposition would do much better. I do not blame the Congress newspapers for consistently misrepresenting the most benevolent Government measures, for declaring that Lord Elgin was indifferent to the death of "millions of India's children" during the famine, or for dwelling at inordinate length on individual instances of English haughtiness; these papers are but consistently carrying out the principles upon which popular government is everywhere conducted. But I do unhesitatingly blame a policy, which, when pushed to its logical conclusion, has brought about the deplorable state of feeling at present existing between the English and the educated classes of Bengal.

The Municipal elections have set strife between the Hindus and Muhamadans; the popular movements conducted through the press and on the platform have estranged the English and the most educated classes of native society, and have added to the bitterness of Hindu and Muhamadan rivalry; it has been left to the English to bring discredit on the most venerable of free institutions, and to prove how unsuitable trial by jury is to a country of mixed nationalities. The people of India commonly say that no Englishman has yet been hanged for the murder of a native. It is an ugly fact which it is no use to disguise that the murder of natives by Englishmen is no infrequent occurrence. In one issue of the Amrita Bazar Patrika of this month (August 11th, 1898,) three contemporary cases are dealt with, in none of which have the prisoners paid the full legal penalty for murder. I cannot pretend to an opinion whether in these or previous cases there has been an actual miscarriage of justice, but I do unhesitatingly assert that very few Englishmen in India believe that an English jury, as juries are at present constituted, would even on the clearest evidence convict one of their countrymen of the murder of a native. The pick of Anglo-Indian society is either not qualified or exempted from serving on a jury; juries in European cases are therefore empanelled from among English shopkeepers or railway employés of the big towns; this is the very class in which the arrogance of a conquering race is most offensively strong, and their moral sense does not endorse the legal theory that an Englishman should atone with his life for killing a "nigger". When three artillery men were sentenced by the Chief Justice to seven years' rigorous imprisonment for having brutally caused the death of a respectable practitioner (Dr. Suresh Chandra) in Barrackpore, an English military officer wrote anonymously to one of the native papers approving the verdict and declaring that in any other part of the world but India, the three artillerymen would have been hanged. Upon this, one of the English papers, "The Morning Post", retorted: "We should like to have the name of this individual. Without it, we must decline to believe that there is any Britisher in this country, *so degenerate as to subscribe to such sentiments.*" (The italics are mine.)

Juries in all countries are liable to be swayed by passion or prejudice, but such a miscarriage of justice in India begets political evil; the people are irritated against the Government because they do not believe that the laws are evenly administered. A villager once said to me: "How is it, sahib, that, if one of your people kills one of us, nothing is done to him; yet if we but lift a stone against you we are punished?" And the evil is increased by the partisan spirit in which such cases are dealt with by the different sections of the press, as the Amrita Bazar Patrika (Aug. 14th, 1898) shows in the following extract, which seems to me both temperate and true: "Whenever a case of the murder of an Indian by a European is brought to notice, the Anglo-Indian papers, as a rule, ignore it. But they can do better by noticing it and pointing out the favourable points, if there be any, on behalf of the accused. If there be none, they can yet remove much of the prejudice against the offender by expressing disapprobation of his conduct, and sympathy for the relations of the accused. One line from the 'Pioneer', observing that the Barrackpore offenders should thank their stars for having been able to get off so cheap, reconciled the Indians to the lenient sentences passed upon the accused more than even the remarks of the Chief Justice to the same effect. The Anglo-Indian papers, by ignoring such cases, throw upon the Indian papers the task of commenting upon them. The result is that these cases are sometimes commented upon with bitterness, and the gulf between the races is thus widened. If such cases are noticed and dealt with in a spirit of fairness by the Anglo-Indian papers, the Indians will feel it a duty to treat them with more charity."

The introduction of free institutions into India has been a mistake because they have thrown discord and division among the peoples whom it was our duty to reconcile. And India is not an isolated example of the failure of popular methods in an unsuitable environment. We may judge to what a catastrophe we have been steering, by contemplating the difficulties in which the Austro-Hungarian monarchy is floundering. The Emperor Franz-Josef has tried the experiment of what is hastily termed "liberalism", and he has found that the Germans, Magyars, Bohemians, Poles, Croatians, Italians and the rest have aggravated their pretensions to separate national autonomy under the parliamentary *régime;* these pretensions are in the nature of things incapable of satisfaction, but men's minds have been so embittered by mutual recrimination in the press and in the Chamber that it is doubtful whether they will resign them without civil war. Surely it is an abuse of words to apply the term "liberal" to a policy which leads directly to such a catastrophe as this. Unless its use as a party badge has deprived the word of all honourable signification, it would be more legitimate to apply the term "liberal" to a policy which tends to create (not to destroy) a national sentiment within the circle of which self-government would be possible. It would, to my thinking, be legitimate to use the word in describing the policy which has done so much for the progress of Mexico. "President Porfirio Diaz saw that what Mexico needed was strong personal rule to lift the country out of chaos. Worshippers of formulas will condemn every step Diaz has taken: those who look at political and social results will justify most steps. We are not dealing, be it remembered, with a country of centuries of settled life and ordered institutions, but with the vast regions which had to be reclaimed from ignorance, violence, and barbarism. Stern work was needed to attain the end, and President Diaz did not shrink from it. He suppressed the newspapers, as Signor Crispi suppressed them in Italy, because they made for the disruption of a nation which was becoming compact and unified." (The Progress of Mexico, the "Spectator", Feb. 19th, 1898.)

It is apparently necessary for English politicians to behold a country given up to anarchy before they can realise that popular institutions make for the disruption of a nation which is not yet compact and unified. If they looked beneath the delusive calm which the army maintains in India, they would behold all the passions which beget civil war, unscotched by a hundred years of unwilling peace.

CHAPTER III

ON THE FORMATION OF NATIONALITIES

I HAVE argued that if India is ever to govern herself it can only be on condition that she grows into a nation; it does not matter to my present purpose whether we should desire the creation of one or two or several nationalities; the important thing is that the people who inhabit one locality should be knit to each other by firmer bonds than the links of sympathy which unite them to the inhabitants of other countries; the continent of India may be split up into as many nationalities as Europe and yet be self-governing in the sense that a foreign yoke would not be indispensable to save her from anarchy. What is important is that each unit, such as Bengal or the Punjab, should be conterminous with a national sentiment. How is this sentiment to be generated?

At the outset we are confronted with the difficulty that it is by no means easy to define what constitutes a nation. A people may talk different languages, come of different races and follow different religions and yet form but one nation, as is evident from the anomalous case of Switzerland. Renan thought nationality sprang "from community of historical antecedents"; it is true that the people who have been associated with each other in the past have generally ended by growing into one nation. Renan's definition does not in reality introduce a fresh idea, but is rather a generalization which includes various subordinate elements of nationality; a common language, for instance, generally implies a common literature, and a literature, which is a common inheritance from the past, will make the people conscious of a unity of historical traditions. But this definition fails us in the case of those perplexing countries which, in spite of a community of historical antecedents, have shown no tendency to evolve a national sentiment. Why, for instance, is there no Austrian nationality? Why none in the Ottoman Empire?

It must be conceded that different countries have arrived at the conception of nationality in different ways, and all ways are not equally practicable for India. The patriotism of the oligarchic states of the classical world was largely based on the myth of an eponymous ancestor, and religious zeal has often fused into one tribes that had previously lived perpetually at war; but the senior members at least of the Indian Civil Service will hardly think themselves qualified to pose as divine lawgivers; and for them the case of France offers a more practical analogy. The most perfect nationality in the world has been fashioned by quite intelligible historic causes and in spite of geographical difficulties as great as those of India. The kings of France were the smiths who forged a nation out of the diverse elements which distracted the country, and it is instructive to consider why they succeeded where the house of Hapsburg failed. The aim of Louis XI or Louis XIV was to be King of France, and they did not alter their pretensions when they added new provinces to the kingdom. But the Hapsburgs were never content to be Archdukes of Austria; they were haunted by the phantom of world-wide supremacy to which the title of Emperor was a perpetual pretension; they would have derogated had they limited their ambitions to the glories of the kings of France; they ruled indeed over a sufficiently well-defined area, but in such a sort that their title was not impaired, but rather bettered by the diversity of the subject peoples; for it was the diversity and not the homogeneity of their subjects which best accorded with their pretensions. It is owing to a similar ambition that the Sultan of Turkey has failed to evoke a sentiment of nationality in his subjects. As titular head of the Muhamadan world, he claims the allegiance of Muhamadans outside his own frontiers, and he cannot be satisfied with the obedience of the subjects over whom he rules directly. Had he ever identified his glories with a particular tract of country, the receding flood of Muhamadan dominion would not now reveal the embryo nationalities of Eastern Europe in the same condition as before they were overwhelmed.

These cases point to the defect in Renan's definition. Similarity of historical antecedents does not of itself bind peoples together; their association in the past must have been of a nature to unite them for common action and to move them to common enthusiasm. The passive subjects of a common conqueror have similar historical associations, but the recollections of servitude suggest no inspiring memories. There are possibly two cases in which foreign conquest may promote the growth of national feeling; the first is when the subject peoples unite to throw off the stranger's yoke, in which case they found a nationality on the ruins of his empire; the bond that knits them together is their association in a glorious struggle. The second case is when the conqueror so identifies himself with the people he has subjected that they take his glories as their own. India herself has once welcomed such a conqueror. Akbar induced the Rajput and the Pathan to resign their petty hopes of independent glory by offering them a share in a greater empire which they themselves helped to build. This policy, short-lived though it was, (for it was reversed by his great grandson Aurangzeb,) bore splendid fruit; the northern half of India, which was Akbar's empire in Hindustan still cherishes the memory of the Moghul reign, and it is to-day more straitly united by common associations than the provinces of southern India. Akbar's example is both a warning and encouragement to us who are his successors. It is ridiculous to ascribe his success solely to his policy of toleration; people will not love a foreigner merely because he lets them alone; as a Bengali paper recently said, the Hindus venerate the memory of Akbar because he made Hindus governors of provinces; in other words even the conquered races can take a pride in the glories of the Moghul Empire which conferred lustre upon themselves as well as the house of Tamarlane.

If a conqueror practises a different religion to the majority of his subjects and is determined to reserve the privileges of command to the followers of his own creed, his best policy will be to convert, by force if necessary, all his subjects to that creed; by that means he will secure a homogeneous empire. This was the great mistake of the Ottoman rulers, that they forbore from converting their Christian subjects last century, when a little judicious pressure would have herded them all into the Muhamadan fold. Two policies were open to the Sultan of Turkey; he might have withdrawn all peculiar privileges from the Muhamadans and placed himself at the head of the Bulgarians, Greeks, and Turks within his borders, and contented himself with being the sovereign of one of the fairest countries of the earth; or he might have ruled as a

Muhamadan monarch over a purely Muhamadan kingdom and set himself to the extirpation of heretics. As a matter of fact he maintained the special privileges of his co-religionists, but left unmolested the Christians who were to conspire with his enemies in the day of his weakness. His Christian Majesty, Ferdinand the Catholic, understood his trade better, and created special machinery, which proved extremely effective, for securing uniformity of religious opinion in Spain.

We cannot of course obtain immunity from religious strife by forcibly converting all India to Christianity, and it may be mentioned parenthetically that such a course would not nowadays solve our political difficulties, because the love which Christians bear to one another in India is not strong enough to overcome the prejudices of race. But the lesson to be learned from history is sufficiently clear. The Government which wishes to create a national spirit must be based upon a principle which its subjects can reciprocate, it must place before the people a conception of Government which will evoke their enthusiastic loyalty. In a country in which race, language and religion tend to divide, the people must be provided with a central idea which will unite them all, to which they can all be equally loyal and round which the feeble beginnings of nationality can cluster. Does the British rule in India provide the people with such an idea? Most emphatically, No.

The basis, both in theory and practice, of our Empire is the supremacy of the British race, and this is not an idea for which anybody but ourselves can feel any enthusiasm. The fact that our Indian Empire is founded upon the domination of the English race is so obvious as to need no demonstration; it is in all men's mouths, in all the papers, and it is the only principle upon which we act consistently. The body which ultimately governs India is the House of Commons, and the House of Commons represents the English people, therefore the people of India are the subjects of the English Electorate. In India itself there is no likelihood of any one forgetting the ascendency of the English race. "You are the conquerors and we are the conquered", is a phrase often on the lips of the people. "Yes", says the better class of Englishmen, "but we are all equal before the law". Englishmen of the baser sort say with considerable logical consistency: "Let Government take up a courageous attitude; we are the dominant race and intend to remain so; all the privileges of conquest should be reserved for us." These are the men who will not allow a native to carry an umbrella over his head in their presence, and insist that every native shall salaam to them, though such men have rarely the courtesy to acknowledge the salute. A case acquired a certain notoriety of late, and is said to have gone up to the Secretary of State, in which an Englishman thrashed an old native schoolmaster, not because he had neglected to salute him, but because the salaam was not performed with that inclination from the vertical which the Englishman thought was due to the dominant caste.

This is not a principle of Government which the people can reciprocate, and therefore we have failed to elicit any warm sentiment of loyalty. Englishmen like to argue that because we have conferred many material benefits upon the people of India, because we have substituted good government for anarchy, therefore they ought to be loyal to us; and many who recognise the obvious fact that the people are not enthusiastically grateful to us, imagine that it is due to certain abuses in our government at which the people are repining. It would be a sufficient answer to say that the people do not acknowledge that our rule has been beneficial to them. They do not vividly realize the miseries of anarchy from which British rule has saved them; and they are apt to idealize a time when a man could feed himself and his family for a rupee; when the rites of their own religion were celebrated with pomp and splendour, and to contrast this Iron Age, (Kali Yug) with the good days of old. The widely read Bangavasi of 26th June, 1897, observed, "The stately swan has ceased to disport himself on the cool and pellucid waters of the village pond, and pujas and festivals, dances and singing, pleasures and amusements, and sky-rending laughter are all gone. Clad in another's clothes, holding umbrellas not our own and supporting ourselves by begging, we are now leading the lives of slaves and beggars." As a survey of the economic condition in the past and the present, I do not think the above of much value. I believe that British rule has enormously increased the material prosperity of India, but that historical fact will not make the people loyal unless they themselves believe that they are better off. As a matter of fact the belief is almost universal that India has been impoverished by British rule.

But even if we could convince the people that they are now better off than they were a century ago and that the evils they are suffering from are due to economic causes beyond the control of Government, would that belief make them loyal? Experience certainly does not support the idea that people are loyal to a government in proportion to the material advantages which they derive from it. The citizens of the United States are enthusiastically loyal to a Constitution under which their business is shamefully mismanaged; the Royalists who followed the House of Stuart into exile were probably under no illusions with regard to the administration of Charles I, or the second James. Loyalty is essentially a generous sentiment which induces the nobler portion of mankind to sacrifice life and property for the sake of a particular family or cause, and it will not be evoked by a statistical comparison of the present with the past even if the calculation shews a nett balance in favour of the present.

My contention is that because our administration is based upon the domination of the English race, a principle which can be inspiring only to Englishmen, it has failed to rouse in the people of India warm devotion to our Empire; whereas it was our duty so to administer India as to beget a loyalty for the central government ardent enough to induce the different sections of Indian society to associate in support of a common idea. By recognizing the obligation to an allegiance higher than the claims of religion or kindred they would have grown familiar with a conception of public duty co-extensive with the continent of India; this conception of public duty, encouraged and strengthened by immemorial tradition, might have one day been found to have developed into a sentiment of Indian nationality.

It remains for me to prove in the next chapter that there is a principle which we might put forward as the ostensible basis of our Empire, of which no Englishman need be ashamed, and which would command the enthusiastic veneration of the people of India.

CHAPTER IV

THE EMPRESS OF INDIA

OWING to the ascendency of democracy in the civilized world, the services which the institution of monarchy has rendered to mankind are imperfectly rocognised in modern speculations on the art of government; yet the political value of these services can hardly be overrated. In unsettled countries society has two needs which no other form of government is so well fitted to satisfy as monarchy. Primitive society needs firstly a bond of allegiance which shall be equally binding on all its heterogeneous members; secondly, it is needful in such a society that loyalty to the central government should be openly and assiduously fostered. Monarchy satisfies both these requirements because, in the first place, devotion to the person of a sovereign is a simple and easily intelligible sentiment to which almost all men are prone, and in countries in which men are divided by race, language, and religion, obedience to the wishes of one man is almost the only form of allegiance which appeals strongly to all alike. This sentiment is starved in the self-governing communities of Western Europe, but those who were present at the Jubilee and witnessed the hurricane of emotion which swept along the streets of London at the sight of the Queen will not readily believe that it is altogether dead in England. Yet we must go to unsettled countries where the sovereign is the only refuge from anarchy to understand the proportions to which this sentiment can attain. East of Suez, where, according to Mr. Kipling, "there ain't no ten commandments", there lies upon the eyes and foreheads of all men a law which is not found in the European Decalogue; and this law runs: "Thou shall honour and worship the man whom God shall set above thee for thy king; if he cherish thee thou shalt love him; and if he plunder and oppress thee thou shalt still love him, for thou art his slave and his chattel."

The second advantage of monarchy is that it directly fosters loyalty to the central government. The sovereign confers his favours upon his own friends and entrusts political power only to those whom he believes sincerely attached to his person. In democratic countries the public conscience is shocked at the "Spoils System" because the politicians who employ the resources of the commonwealth for the benefit of a faction profess to consult the good of the universal people; but where the king *is* the state, the highest public duty of his servants consists in consolidating his power, and his ministers will not be blamed if they use the influence which their position in the state gives them to promote the interests of his friends and to discourage those who wish to upset his government. And as the favour of the king is the principal avenue to dignity and wealth, the most ambitious and able men of the country will gravitate towards the court; those who find favour in the king's eyes will rise to positions in which they can influence public opinion; whereas those who, like Mons. de Montespan, cannot endorse the king's view of his own behaviour, are banished from court and sink into insignificance. In this way the court not only becomes the natural home of loyalty, but at the same time the capital of the kingdom, the intellectual centre from which the ideas start that eventually permeate public opinion throughout the country. Thus the partiality of the king in the choice of his servants, which is the natural result of autocracy, tends, if it is not grossly abused, to render popular and so strengthen the central government without which a nation can hardly come into being. When the ablest and most influential men of the country are to be found in the king's court, the court leads public opinion in the country, and a court is necessarily loyal because those who contend for the king's smile are not likely to find fault with his administration or to disapprove of a policy which he has sanctioned. Monarchy has from its very essence this advantage over democracy, that whereas the demagogue wins to power by expatiating to the sovereign people upon the multitude of their grievances which the existing government has failed to redress, even the most opposite factions at court will vie with each other in protesting their satisfaction with the existing constitution.

India is a country in which the advantages of a monarchical form of government are brought into the clearest relief; it would be impossible to find any general principle of coherence, other than monarchy, which would unite all the sections of Indian society. There are white men, and brown men, and black men in India; there are fire-worshippers and Muhamadans, Christians and Hindus, Sikhs and Jains; there is a very jungle of languages with a bewildering undergrowth of dialects, and not only does each considerable tract of country speak a distinct language, but almost every language has an alphabet of its own. What political formula can be devised that would cover them all? It is only in obedience to one great master that all can unite without heart-burning. And as monarchy is the only form of government suitable to India, it is also the only form of government for which she has shewn any aptitude. The history of India is singularly barren in political ideas; a small Greek state was richer in speculation on political principles than the whole continent of India has ever been. The one elevating conception which gives a pathetic interest to the weary tale of bloodshed which is known as Indian history, is the faithfulness of the followers to the hand that gives them salt. The memory of the Moghul Empire after a hundred and fifty years of anarchy and foreign dominion, still lives in the hearts of the people. I have seen a wandering puppet-show representing the court of Akbar, in which, by a quaint anachronism, English Mem Sahibs and Padrés joined with Indian Rajahs and the Sultan of Rum (Constantinople,) in doing homage to the Great Moghul. For about a century the house of Tamerlane claimed the allegiance of their Indian subjects irrespective of race or creed; after this the policy of Akbar was reversed by Aurangzeb, whose puritanical zeal re-opened the old wounds. But in this brief period they succeeded in creating an impression upon public opinion, comparable to the effect produced on men's minds by the long line of Roman Emperors. As the Imperial purple continued to cast its spell on the minds of the barbarians who had carved themselves principalities out of the Roman Empire, so the tradition of the Empire of Delhi lingered; and the Emperors, though reduced to impotence, remained the fountain of legality from which English traders and Jat plunderers were glad to draw a title to their booty. I have been told that, in the days of Lord Ellenborough, a certain Hindu Rajah sent a notable wrestler in his service to wrestle before the Emperor of Delhi, then a pensioner of the East India Company; the Emperor was so pleased with his performance that, with his own hands, he fastened a band of gold upon his head. When the wrestler came back, the Rajah and his court rose to do honour to the man who carried a token of the imperial favour, and each in turn did obeisance to the band which had been touched by the hands of Akbar's successor.

The native states illustrate the value of monarchical institutions in India. It can hardly be contended that an overwhelming proportion of the native chiefs of to-day are born leaders of men; in the regularity of their lives and in their sense of public duty they certainly have no advantage over the collectors and commissioners of British India. But the native chiefs have achieved success in one of the most important functions of statesmanship, in which the highly educated Civil Service has failed: they have won the loyalty of their people. This cannot be attributed to the fact that they are natives of the soil, for, in the states where loyalty is most conspicuous, the chiefs are foreigners who do not talk the language of the people. Holkar, Sindhia, and the Gaekwar are Mahrattas; they and their courts speak Mahratti which is not intelligible to the majority of their subjects. The Nizam is a Muhamadan who speaks Urdu; whereas his subjects are chiefly Hindus whose native tongue is Telegu or Canarese or Mahratti. Nor have any of these dynasties an older title than ourselves to the homage of the people of India; they and almost all the reigning chiefs won their thrones in the anarchy which followed the downfall of the Moghul Empire. That they have succeeded in winning the loyalty of their people is solely due to the natural advantages of the monarchical form of government in India. They have not asked their subjects to assent to any general principle of government, for none of universal application could have been found, but they have claimed their fealty to the person of the monarch. And in the second place they have never pretended to be neutral upon political questions, but have employed all the resources of the state in support of a particular set of views; this policy gives one party such an ascendency in the state that a conflict is out of the question. I once asked a very experienced Political Agent what he believed to be the reason why "cow-killing riots" never occur in native states, and the answer he gave contains, I think, the true explanation. The reason is that, upon this question, the chief himself always holds a very decided opinion, and all the forces of the state are arrayed upon one side or the other; a Muhamadan chief of course allows the slaughter of kine, a Hindu Rajah of course prohibits it; so the question is settled.

That the native chiefs do possess the affection of their subjects to a very remarkable degree cannot be doubted by any one who has ever resided in a native state. If any tourist who comes to study the East on a three months' trip, wishes to enter into the political ideas of the people of India and at the same time to see one of the most picturesque sights which India has still to show, let him pay a visit to any petty chief in Rajputana or Bundelkhand, and, when the glare of day has softened to a golden haze and the dusty droves of cattle are returning to their stalls, let him accompany the Rajah on his evening ride. From the gateway of the fort, the Rajah's elephant, in long housings of velvet and cloth of gold, comes shuffling down the steep declivity; on his back, in a silver howdah, sits the Rajah, laden with barbaric pearl and gold; behind him clatter his kinsmen and retainers on brightly caparisoned horses; these horses are, for the most part, pink-nosed, squealing brutes, but they are controlled by a standing martingale and a spiky bit, and make a brave show. As the cavalcade winds down the narrow streets the men pick up their swords and hurry forward; the women and children rush to the doors of their houses, and all the people gaze upon their prince with an expression of almost ecstatic delight; as the elephant passes, each man puts one hand to the ground and shouts "Maharaju Ram Ram". The most indolent tourist cannot fail to notice the joy upon all the people's faces; and when the cavalcade winds home and he realises the intensity of delight which the mere sight of their prince has caused the subjects, he will begin to understand the suitability of monarchy to certain phases of social evolution.

True to their political traditions, the people of India have fastened upon the one aspect of English rule which is in harmony with their own ideals, and have invested the name of the Empress of India with a halo of love and veneration. The Queen has never set foot in India, and her influence over the administration of the country is but shadowy and nominal; and yet the educated classes, the only people, that is, who think upon political questions at all, feel for her person a warmth of loyalty which it would be hard to match in England. The loyalty felt in England for the Queen is an eminently reasonable feeling; it is a mixture of esteem for the virtues of an exalted personage and patriotic pride in the greatness of England. The Queen is to Englishmen a symbol of their world-wide Empire; and the lustiness with which they swell the chorus of "God save the Queen" is at least partly due to its being their National Anthem. But Indian loyalty is not tainted by any selfish feeling of national glorification. I can best characterize it as a tender personal affection. The nearest approach to it in England is to be found in the army, which has naturally preserved many of the traditions of a monarchical state of society. The old Colonel, who murmurs "The Queen, God bless her!" over his port, does entertain a sentiment which is similar in kind to that which her Indian subjects feel; it is a personal, I almost said a private, affection.

If it be remembered that in India, loyalty means devotion to the sovereign, I do not think there is any serious exaggeration in the contention of the "Dainik-o-Somochar Chundrika", that "the Indian people are by nature and by virtue of their religious principles more loyal than Englishmen. Indian loyalty is a hundred times deeper and sincerer than English loyalty. In England the Queen is only a constitutional monarch: in India she is a Goddess incarnate."

Although articles to this effect may be found as thick as blackberries in the vernacular press, I do not think that I should materially strengthen my case by lengthy quotations from the newspapers. Papers in India cannot be trusted to reflect public opinion, and I have only quoted them where I can corroborate their contentions out of my own experience. Moreover, upon this question the journalist actually misrepresents the sentiments of the people, as, while acknowledging the feeling, he generally attempts to find a reason for it in the benefits the Queen has conferred on India; but loyalty is properly a sentiment which is recognised intuitionally, and it gains as little as the cause of virtue by the advocacy of utilitarian reasoning. Perhaps I may be allowed one quotation which is free at least from this error. The Jubilee number of the "Chinsura Vartavaha" contained the following: (20 June, 1897.)

"Come, gods and goddesses, come. Join us in

this universal rejoicing and festivity. India has, so to speak, been turned into heaven, and we are as happy as the immortal gods. We are in fact overpowered with joy on this auspicious occasion, and our heart is full to overflowing. We are singing the praises of Mother Victoria, and let the gods shower flowers on us. Shall we ever see a return of this happy occasion? Shall we ever get such a kind-hearted, benevolent, and generous ruler? Queen Victoria protects us as the Divine Mother. She is more than a human being. She is a goddess. So many virtues can dwell in a goddess, and in a goddess alone.

"We are often accused of want of loyalty. We are blamed for continually harping on our grievances. But, Mother, is it disloyalty to represent our grievances? You have asked us to lay our grievances before you, and this makes us bold enough to complain of oppression and highhandedness when they become really unbearable. In your eyes all your subjects are equal. Mother, when your white children oppress us, shall we not complain against them?"

The House of Commons directs the Queen's ministers to conduct the administration of India in conformity with the political principles which have proved beneficial in England, and it has never been to the trouble of considering whether these principles are equally acceptable to the people of India. But the continuity of history can never be safely disregarded. We have not based our dominion upon principles which commend themselves to the political instincts of the people, and hence our government has failed to take root in the country; it rests upon the top of the people and, by its massive weight, keeps them in their places and prevents commotion, but it draws no nourishment from the soil, and the people have not come to look upon it as a part of themselves. If a great statesman ever had the opportunity of remodelling the constitution of India and, like Napoleon, of constructing the whole edifice of government afresh, he would assuredly seize upon the loyalty of the people to the Queen as the cardinal fact upon which to found the fabric of Empire; he would recognize that the Queen is beyond all comparison the greatest political force in India. If anarchy were again let loose in India and all the possible candidates made a bid for supreme power, the Prince of Wales, commissioned by the Queen, would raise a larger force than any antagonist; adherents would flock to him from all parts of the country as soon as he landed in India, and the moral sense of the people would everywhere be on his side; their consciences would admit him as the only rightful claimant.

A statesman who was devising a constitution suitable to India's particular needs would also be bound to recognize that the only conception of civic duty which is deeply impressed upon the

Indian conscience, is the obligation of fidelity to the hand that gives them salt. Owing perhaps to its supreme value to society in a country so divided, faithfulness to the salt has been elevated to the rank of a cardinal virtue in India; namak haram, (faithless to the salt,) is a term expressive of the greatest infamy in a society in which the taking of bribes to pervert justice is considered venial.

Here then is the general principle of which we are in search. Loyalty to the Empress is a sentiment which suggests no humiliating consciousness of subjection to a foreign yoke, a sentiment by which men of the most opposite creeds and races are equally moved, a sentiment peculiarly in accord with the genius of the people of India, and, what is more important than anything else, a sentiment which is already in existence.

CHAPTER V

REGARDING SOME MAXIMS OF POPULAR GOVERNMENT

As the Queen of England is already Empress of India, it may be objected that our Empire in the East is already placed upon the right foundation, and therefore on my own showing no change is required. This objection is not likely to come from anybody who has lived long in India; our dominion is universally recognised as depending on the supremacy of the British race; even in official documents the Queen's name occurs but rarely; hardly any administrative act, except the Proclamation of 1858, is understood to be the expression of her wishes. A machine called Government, of which the principal parts are Englishmen, directs the business of the country according to certain rules and regulations, and the subject who longs for a human personality to love and follow is unable to discover that this machine has any sympathies or antipathies. The natives of India have, so to say, discovered the Queen in our admistration for themselves from their inherent love of a personality and by an instinctive perception of their own requirements. If a part of statesmanship consists in suiting the Government to the temper of the governed, our proper policy would have lain in entrusting the whole direction of Government to the Empress of India.

But before discussing in detail the changes which would nowadays follow upon the substitution of the supremacy of the Crown for the supremacy of race, I must consider the essential difference between the political principles which should govern a monarchy and a modern popular government; for unless this is done I shall be pulled up at every turn by the objection that the changes which I am suggesting are opposed to the most fundamental axioms of English politics.

The political principles of monarchy differ from those which guide popular governments, because the two forms of government are appropriate to different phases in the evolution of society. The great need of primitive society is a central authority to curb the centrifugal forces and promote the unification of the State; and primitive states have almost everywhere adopted monarchy because it was the institution which best satisfied this need. The services which monarchy rendered to European society consisted in crushing aspirants to local independence and in breaking up the groups which resisted assimilation. The kings of Europe succeeded in creating a bond which united the various peoples of their realm and in inducing their subjects to accept it in place of those other bonds which, like religion, do knit men together, but in methods less advantageous to society. This process was perhaps conducted with needless brutality and at the expense of some valuable elements of civilization, yet it was on the whole a salutary process, and Western Europe may to-day be grateful that it has been accomplished. But the institution which most assisted the evolution of the organism at an early stage of development became useless when the State was unified and compacted by a national sentiment running through all its parts; and when an institution has become superfluous its retention is generally harmful and an obstacle to further development. Monarchy having completed in European countries the task for which it was specially adapted, was generally sloughed off and its place taken by institutions more suitable to a later phase of evolution. This constitutional transformation was accompanied by throes and convulsions which have not yet entirely subsided, and our political views are still deeply coloured by reminiscences of the struggle against absolutism. The political maxims by which Europe is governed to-day, are not in reality immutable principles of universal application, but generalizations from contemporary society, to which the political history of the last two centuries has given currency and a certain stamp of intrinsic merit. In the latter half of the eighteenth century, as the industrious Bluntschli observes, "men sought to find some limitation to the over-government of that enlightened despotism, which benevolent as it was, proved oppressive and destructive of personal freedom, and which was accustomed to justify every interference with family life, with the free choice of a career, and with the administration of private revenues by a professed regard for the general welfare. The definition of the end of the State as the maintenance of legal security seemed to offer a convenient weapon for opposing this over-government successfully." That is to say that the application to modern Europe of the conception of the state which is peculiar to primitive society proved harmful, and another conception of the functions of government acquired credit which is proper to a later phase of evolution. In its proper environment I do not quarrel with this view of the state, I only protest against the application of it to India.

Many of the political maxims which are believed to be axiomatic in Europe ultimately rest on the assumption that the inhabitants of the State are a nation. Of this nature are the maxims which relate to party government; in countries in which all classes are equally anxious to maintain the stability of the State it is no doubt desirable that the constitution should allow of the expression of differences of opinion; it is therefore expedient that the resources of the state should not be used on behalf of one set of political views; and to take but one instance, it is a wise provision that the permanent servants of the nation should not publicly associate themselves with one political party. Since the constitution has made provision for differences of opinion upon political questions, it would obviously be unfair to allow the party that temporarily secured control of the government to employ all the resources of the commonwealth in suppressing opinions adverse to itself. In England there is a tacit recognition that this maxim does not apply to all political opinions indiscriminately, but only to those which may be held without danger to the State, for its application is in practice limited to party questions, that is, to those political questions upon which difference of opinion is permitted by the Constitution. A permanent servant of the Crown may not repel attacks upon the Ministry, but he would probably be allowed to censure opinions which threaten to subvert the constitution, and certainly opinions which are a menace to society. A government official, for instance, might with impunity publish an attack upon the doctrines of the anarchists, because those doctrines are a menace to the existing constitution of society, and because they threaten to subvert institutions with regard to which the constitution has not recognized the desirability of a difference of opinion. It is indeed conceivable that a servant of the crown would not be allowed to express his opinion upon some proposals which do involve a change in the constitution, such, for instance, as the abolition of the House of Lords, or the establishment of a republic in England, but that is because no alteration in the technical constitution could shatter the edifice of English society. The English people have learnt so thoroughly how to govern themselves, and the desire to preserve the common weal has so spread to the uttermost fringe of society, that the English could soon accustom themselves to working another form of government as successfully as the present one. Their existence as a nation (apart from external aggression) no longer depends upon the stability of a central authority; the forces of law and order have spread in ever widening circles until they have grown co-extensive with the whole people of Great Britain. This is the real constitution of England, which no manipulation of the law can alter, and hence it is not dangerous to affirm in England that the end of the State is the maintenance of legal security.

This conception of the functions of the State has dominated our policy in India; the government has forbidden its servants to take any part in political movements, and jealously forbids them to influence public opinion; it has tolerated the freest expression of opinion, and it confers posts and dignity with absolute impartiality on those who admire and those who most virulently criticise its administration of Indian affairs. Now the first and most fundamental question of politics which can occur to the recently dethroned Muhamadan and the twice-conquered Hindu is whether or not it is desirable that the British Raj should continue in India. This is exactly one of the cases in which the interest of the individual is not identical with the interests of the greater number. Owing to the existing constitution of Indian society, the answer will vary according to the view taken by each individual of the prospects of his own community; if he is a Muhamadan he will believe that with the help of the Afghan he could regain the lost sceptre of Delhi; if he is a Mahratta he will call to mind that, had it not been for the English, the Peshwa would have laid all India under contribution; there are many Sikhs alive who can remember how their nation lorded it over the Muhamadan peasantry of the Punjab; the Bengali fondly imagines that the reign of brute force is at an end, and that if the English could be persuaded to retire, the task of administering India would devolve upon the Bengalis, as the most educated people of the country.

These forecasts are probably all wide of the mark, but they sufficiently indicate that the assumption which lies at the root of English political maxims cannot be made in India. It is for this reason that I refuse to accept the principles of English politics as axioms in the administration of our Eastern dependency. That they have not been challenged hitherto is due to the fact that our officials in India have imbibed their political principles in Europe, quite as much as to the fact that the English Parliament dictates the policy which they have to carry out.

An instructive example of the way in which Englishmen are misled by the vocabulary of English politics is to be found in the misunderstanding which arises in the use of the word Government. In England the Government generally means the Ministry for the time being in power, and to overthrow the Government is an act quite consistent with loyalty to the Constitution, which provides for this periodic contingency. In India, the Government means the Constitution, and in the whole peninsula there is not a trace of any alternative organization which would save the country from anarchy if the existing government were overthrown; and yet Englishmen are in the habit of speaking as lightly of attacks upon the Government of India as they do of the attempts to substitute one set of English politicians for another equally respectable who would conduct the affairs of the country on practically identical principles.—When Mr. Tilak was sent to prison for saying that non-Hindus (Mlechhas) had not received a firman from Heaven, inscribed on a brazen plate, empowering them to govern India, "Truth" remarked: "If this definition (Mr. Justice Strachey's definition of disaffection) is correct, the law against seditious incitement in India is remarkable. Here in England we are accustomed freely to criticise the action of Government and often in a mode which is the reverse of a disposition to support its measures, and we do this, not only in the Press, but in Parliament. Were the Indian law our law, most of Her Majesty's present Ministers would have been liable to imprisonment for showing this wicked disapprobation of the Government when Mr. Gladstone was at its head and Mr. Morley was the Irish Secretary. Pushed to its full extent, in fact, the ruling of the Indian Judge, if applied to England, would result in each of the two parties of the State conveying to prison the Parliamentary minority and all journalists who might support them."

The Indian administration would be saved from such misunderstandings as this, if it were usual to speak of a certain class of Indian politicians as attempting to subvert the constitution and not merely as desirous of overthrowing the Government, which is after all what half the politicians at home are actually trying to do.

A monarchical government, which I have attempted to show is the form of government appropriate to India, has different functions to fulfil, and has therefore a stock of political maxims special to itself. The grand object of monarchy is to unify, to compel the conflicting elements over which it happens to rule to cohere together. In pursuit of this object the supreme government must not be content to remain a passive spectator of the ferment of public opinion, but must be an energetic partisan, shattering the disruptive forces and aiding the weak beginnings of loyalty and patriotism. The true monarch, like Akbar or Peter the Great, will take upon himself to decide what things are undesirable for his people and what things are desirable, he will use all the forces at his disposal to promote the policy upon which he has decided, and employ his sceptre in one of its primitive uses, as a rod upon the backs of malcontents. It would be repugnant to the sense of a 19th century monarch to coerce opinion by force, but moral persuasion is still at his disposal; he will insist as a condition of service, that all who are in his employment shall hold one set of political views; he will reward certain opinions with wealth and honours, and publicly express his disapproval of any other. He will not be content with using the personal influence of himself and his officers to popularise his policy, but will seize control of the agencies which mould public opinion.

This, of course, is pure autocracy, but until it can be shown that another form of government is equally capable of developing a national sentiment, I shall continue to hold that that policy is most liberal which creates those conditions upon which the very existence of the State depends.

It may be urged that the logical consequence of adopting this theory would be that the Queen of England should start for India and conduct the administration of the country with her own hands. Whether this would be desirable or not is scarcely worth discussing, for it is obviously impossible. A despot who, like Aurangzeb, personally superintends the administration, needs to give all his nights and days to the task of governing India. Although nobody doubts the high ideal of public duty which inspires the English Royal family, it is obvious that the sovereign cannot be spared from her other duties for what is after all but a fraction of the Empire. But, as a matter of fact, this sacrifice, even if it could be made, is not necessary. The native chiefs, who have been more successful than ourselves in evoking the loyalty of their subjects, leave most of the management of their States to ministers, and are not even seen by many of their subjects outside the capital; but the administration is known to be conducted according to their wishes; they can interfere when they like, and what is most important of all, the resources of the state are openly employed to further their private desires. To the Indian mind this is the proper fountain of law, and the motto of Indian statesmanship would run: *Voluntas regis suprema lex.* I am altogether of the opinion that it would be desirable to make the Queen's nominal right to direct the administration of India a practical right which she should constantly exercise; that it would be desirable that the hand of the Queen should be felt in the government. But it would be useless for an Anglo-Indian to propose the reversal of the policy which England has followed for over a hundred years; we who are disfranchised and discredited by living in heathen lands need not trouble ourselves to make suggestions that would embroil the fray of parties at home. The House of Commons would certainly discuss this constitutional question like all other questions with a view to its effect upon English politics, and the advantage to India of a certain line of policy would be subordinated to the probable repercussion of that policy upon domestic affairs. That this might be very important I do not deny. "Free nations," said Froude, "cannot govern subject provinces," and it is conceivable that England may one day provide an illustration of the truth of this aphorism. If an imperial sentiment were once vigorously ascendant in English politics, I can believe that for the better governing of our dependencies we would be willing to forego some of the liberties which impede our sway in India, and a generous desire to free our Indian subjects from the humiliation of a foreign yoke might lead us by a very passable logic to the alternative either of shuffling off the responsibility of governing India, or of submitting ourselves to a form of government which would not be degrading to them. Such, at one time, appeared to be the point of view of the Little England party, but from this easily defensible position they have been frightened by a derisory nickname. However, in the suggestions which I make here, I have purposely refrained from an incursion into English politics, not because I feel that the complacency with which the House of Commons regards its management of the Empire is shared in India, but because I know that it is impossible for me to find any argument strong enough to persuade the House to part with its right to meddle. I remain none the less of the opinion that if we are ever to raise our rule in India into that plane of ideas which can command the self-respecting loyalty of the people, it is essential that they should be freed from their dependence upon a body which professes to be but a miniature of England.

In the succeeding chapters I have therefore confined myself to suggesting alterations which are within the competence of the Government of India, if it once can obtain the sanction of the House of Parliament for putting a new complexion upon our dominion in India. Although we love to grumble at the vagaries of the elect of the nation, we do not, even in the East, doubt the conscientious intention of acting justly which inspires the English Commons. In my opinion there is no reason to dread a thorough examination by the House of the fundamental principles upon which India ought to be governed, because, upon sufficiently momentous occasions, the House is capable of discussing first principles in a statesmanlike spirit; but what is to be dreaded is the accidental criticism of individual acts of Indian administration; because it is inevitable that upon such occasions the matter under discussion would be tried by the canons which alone are familiar to English politicians.

CHAPTER VI

PUBLIC OPINION IN INDIA

IF the real authority of the Empress is recognised as the basis of the Government of India, her servants in the East must abandon the maxim that the end of the State is the maintenance of legal security, and adopt in its place a maxim to the effect that the end of the State is the unification of its discordant elements. One then of the principal duties of government will be to influence and guide public opinion, and to accept without timidity or reservation the rôle of educator in regard to the affairs of this world, our own uncertainty with regard to the next being sufficient reason for leaving it to private judgment.

Although we are dealing with a population of nearly 300 million souls, the control of public opinion in India is not so impossible a task as it at first appears. Public opinion exists only in the professional classes, including government servants, in the landed aristocracy and their immediate dependants and the learned or religious classes.

Although I would not commit myself to the opinion that all these have completely mastered the alphabet, they may be taken to coincide roughly with the 15 million * persons returned in the last census as able to read and write. Among these men there is some discussion of public questions and criticism of government measures, and they are conscious to a greater or less extent of their own ability to modify the course of public events. Owing to the division of Indian society into so many water-tight compartments there is no uniform public opinion flowing through all these classes; each community has its own point of view and therefore a public opinion of its own. But yet from among these 15 millions originate the political views which move India; below them is the great body of patient cultivators who accept changes of government with the same resignation as the alternations of the seasons, and would as little presume to meddle with the constitution of government as with the progress of the monsoon. To them the tax-gatherer and drought are alike manifestations of that occult maleficent power which vulgar Hinduism is chiefly concerned to propitiate. In all cases they would follow their natural leaders who are to be found among the 15 millions referred to: either, that is to say, the man of religion who interprets to them the divine will, or the big landowner who

* 15,292,750 men, women and children.

could call the countryside to arms. In considering measures for influencing opinion in India we need therefore only take account of some 15 million people, and these are exactly the persons over whom the Government, as at present constituted, has the greatest influence. In the first place the most respected and influential members of this society are the native officials, the native officers who glitter in the coveted uniforms of the British army, and the Deputy-Collectors and Tahsildars who actually collect the revenue, and convey the orders of Government to villages and rural townlets. These men are respected, not only because of the great power they exercise for good or evil, but because of their immense superiority to the bulk of village society. Government service is a great education in that it takes men away from the petty gossip of the village circle, trains them in the methodical discharge of responsible duties, and brings them into contact with superior minds. My own experience has been that if I go into a small townlet and meet the leading men, I can, after half an hour's talk, pick out those who have been in Government service by their superior intelligence and mental grasp. In attempting therefore to influence opinion we have already this in our favour, that the servants of the Empress are among the natural leaders of Indian society. In the second place it must be remembered that Indian society is almost entirely agricultural, and it is by the agricultural classes that the power of the Government is felt most directly; this is due to the periodic revision of the land revenue settlements and to the fact that the officials possess the right arbitrarily to remit, though not to enhance, the land tax. The landed aristocracy, in particular, are more amenable in India than elsewhere to the wishes of government, because their revenues are derived entirely from land and because they covet titles and decorations from the State, the only means they recognise of adding to their social importance. In the third place, Government service is universally recognised in India as the most honourable career for a man of good family; a similar tradition, to the effect that the Army, the Navy or the Church are the only professions for a gentleman, still lingers, though much discredited, in England; and in India, though work is not held in honour, the service of the State is yet felt to confer lustre on an old and wealthy family. In old days Government service was not only an honour, but also the quickest road to fortune, and though, owing to the growth of money incomes in other professions, it has ceased to be the most lucrative career in India, still the salaries paid by the British Government make the servants of the State comparatively wealthy men in their own society, and are a great attraction to young men starting in life. Owing therefore to these three causes, (1) the social importance of Government officials, (2) the influence of Government over the agricultural classes, and (3) the universal desire to enter Government service, the Government has it in its power to exercise a moulding and modifying influence upon the public opinion of the upper classes of India.

But this power has never yet been used by the Government to strengthen its own position. In the same way as it has never courted popularity, it has never attempted to modify the political opinions of the people in its own favour; it has maintained a consistent attitude of Olympian indifference to the feelings which it inspires in the subject population. As a matter of fact, I believe that for some time past Government has been receding in the esteem of the upper classes. I do not at all wish to be thought to suggest that there is much active discontent, and that disloyalty is rampant in India; that is an alarmist exaggeration to which too much credit was given at the time of the plague riots and Mr. Tilak's conviction. The tone of native opinion might, I think, be more truly described as one of cold and rather unsympathetic criticism of Government; without having any desire to overthrow the existing administration the people are by no means enthusiastic about it.

If the natives of India may be trusted, (I am not sure that their opinion upon a matter of history is necessarily correct,) these were not always the feelings with which the British Raj was regarded. The late Sir Syed Ahmad Khan Bahadur, who was born in 1818 and who was incomparably the greatest authority upon Indian politics of modern times, used to say that the affection with which the people regarded their English officials had very seriously diminished in the last 40 or 50 years; that at the time of the Mutiny the country people were almost always on the side of the English, and the villagers concealed and handed on many Englishmen whom the mutinous Sepoys would have murdered; but he believed that the feeling had greatly changed in recent years, and for that reason he thought the present outlook very gloomy. This I give as a very prevalent opinion upon which no Englishman, perhaps no man living, can venture to speak with confidence.

Now up to a certain point this decline of our administration in popular favour was intrinsically probable and need not lead us to think that the heroic breed of Lawrences and Napiers is lost. When a province is first brought under British rule the existing generation has a very lively sense of the superiority of British over the former administration, and is effusively grateful to a Government which confers on the subject the unfamiliar blessings of security, justice, good roads and an equitable system of taxation; but when the men have passed away who were brought up in misrule and oppression, the succeeding generations look upon good government as a matter of course, not as an unusual blessing calling for peculiar gratitude. I imagine that for some years to come the inhabitants of Omdurman will apprehend the advantages of the English system of government more intelligently than the educated young Egyptian; and in his turn the grey-bearded Fellah, who has hardly yet got over his surprise at receiving payment for working on an embankment for the State, understands what is meant by an oppressive government with more accuracy than a graduate of the Allahabad University. But the memory of no man living in Madras or Bengal runs back to the time when life and property were not secure, and the Bengali and Madrasi feel as little disposed to be grateful to Government for this as a man who has never known sickness feels for his robust health. Englishmen will not realise this, and they expect the people of Bengal to be perennially thankful to us for not ruling them in the same manner as Surajud Doulah; this in the nature of things is impossible; long familiarity with good government must inevitable dull men's appreciation of its value.

But the degree of coolness with which the people regard the British rule to-day is something more than familiarity will explain; and there is a cause at work which would in time destroy a more robust affection than we ever inspired. That cause may be described as follows: The Government of India is always exposed to hostile criticism and is never vigorously defended. For this our pseudo-liberal policy is directly responsible; we have given the people a free press and the express right to comment, either in print or on the platform, upon the measures of Government, but at the same time we have forbidden Government servants to take part in politics, and as practical politics are only differences of opinion upon the policy of Government, this means nothing but that they are forbidden to defend the official policy if it happens to be attacked. This was meant to be free government to the extent of one-half of the principle at least; but we never asked ourselves how it would work without its proper complement in the party system. In a country governed by alternating parties, the Opposition leads and stimulates the discontent against the Ministry for the time being, until, beneath the prolonged cannonade of hostile criticism, the Ministry loses the confidence of the country and resigns; but the English constitution has provided for this periodic overthrow of the Government, and without commotion the leaders of the Opposition are installed in its place and called upon to show that they can direct the affairs of the country better. The mere knowledge that they may at any moment be called upon to make their words good has a sobering effect upon the criticism of the Opposition, and they will generally be chary of making political capital out of evils which it is beyond the power of any government to remedy. All governments must at some time or other lay themselves open to damaging criticism, and the comparison of the oscillation of electoral favour in England to the swing of a pendulum seems to imply that no government can withstand criticism indefinitely. But the Government of India is always in office, it can never challenge its critics to show that they could govern the country better; and the Opposition, secure in their immunity from making their charges good, create ill-will against the Government by laying to its door economic evils which are beyond the cure of state-craft. But although the Government in India is in a position which would certainly be untenable in a democratic country, it is further handicapped by being expressly forbidden to defend its own policy as soon as it is in dispute. Is there any statesman in England who would take office on condition that neither he nor any of his colleagues should answer the charges of the Opposition; that they should never defend or explain their policy, that they should have no organs in the press to fight their battles? Every politician knows that a Ministry so denuded of support could not enjoy the confidence of the nation for a twelvemonth; because in no country of Europe is there a public so judicial and dispassionate as to be able to judge wisely and truly in the face of unchallenged misrepresentation and unrebuked detraction. This seems to me so indisputable that the wonder is that the tide of disaffection against the Government has not risen higher in India. The explanation, I think, is to be found in the indifference of the people to what we call politics. In recent years, however, under the guidance of newspapers in sympathy with the Congress movement, an interest in political questions has been awakened, and with that growing interest the unpopularity of the British Government is rising at an accelerating pace.

In the main, then, I ascribe the present unpopularity of Government to this, that it is subjected to a continuous fire of irresponsible criticism to which it has no opportunity of replying. This evil is permanent and fundamental and will not be removed until our Indian policy is directed on consistent principles either of popular government or of autocracy; the anomalous combination of the two must infallibly produce the result of which we are actually complaining. It is because this evil is so deep-seated and so constant that I have given it prominence here, but I am aware that other reasons are often alleged for the estrangement of the people from their rulers, which I believe in a secondary degree have contributed to the untoward result.

The reason generally given in native society is that the Civilians of to-day neither know the people as well nor feel for them the same patriarchal affection as the Collectors did in earlier times. Old men relate how in their boyhood the Collector or Deputy-Commissioner lived twenty years in a district and knew the domestic history of every important family in the place, and the landed gentry held him in the same respect as a parent, and called him their father or uncle (chacha). Sir Syed Ahmad used often to tell stories illustrating the goodwill that existed in those days between the officials and country gentlemen, and he generally would wind up with his favourite paradox, "Steamers and railways have ruined India;" meaning thereby that rapidity of communication has made England so accessible from India that modern Civilians never get completely severed from Europe and therefore never look upon India as their home.

Englishmen, too, are apt to moralise upon the decay of the Collector's authority. "Why, in the old days," they say, "the Collector was an autocrat and was feared and loved by all the people of the countryside; nowadays the people know well enough that he can only carry out the orders he receives from head-quarters, and therefore they don't respect him." From the same idea arises the complaint that the present Government is over centralised, and that the Secretariat has encroached upon the sphere proper to the executive officer. I fancy that these explanations are only partially true. Centralisation is a necessary condition of effective organisation; the power of the machine is increased in almost direct proportion to the extent to which it works towards a single end, and the Government of India could as little afford any waste of power as a modern army which is intensely centralised in comparison to the old-fashioned agglomerations of local levies. But I do yet think that much of the blame lies at the door of the Secretariat, for the following reasons:

The Secretariat ought to be the fly-wheel which controls the working of the Government machine; its proper function is to see that the machinery of administration is working smoothly, that each individual is sending in his proper tale of work. The besetting sin of such a body will be to suppose that no work is being well done unless that work is shown in its own tables and reports, and it therefore has a tendency to call for an ever-increasing number of returns. This action of the Secretariat influences the local officer in two ways, firstly by engrossing a great deal of his time in the compilation of reports, and secondly by exaggerating the importance of that part of his work which can be shown in statistical form.

This last cause is, I think, the most serious; the local officer knows that his reputation at head-quarters largely depends upon the reports he sends to the Secretariat, and he will therefore give the greater part of his time and his best energy to the work which figures in the reports. This is felt by the local officers themselves to affect their work prejudicially; one of them recently observed in private: "We get to think less of how the work shall be done than how we shall write about it."

Now I am ready to believe that, with regard to the merely mechanical part of government, the influence of the Secretariat does secure the punctual despatch of business; in doing this the Secretariat has discharged the functions for which it was called into existence. But it is not for the Secretariat to decide which of an officer's duties are the most important, nor how far the whole duty of government consists in the punctual despatch of official business; this is the province of statesmen beneath whose direction the departments work towards certain ends; but owing to the inordinate influence of the Secretariat, a narrow and departmental conception of the functions of government controls the policy of the whole Empire.

Now I believe that a large-minded statesman would recognise that, in such a country as India, one of the duties of Government is to attain popularity, to win the affection and confidence ot the people. This is a legitimate object for any Government to strive after, because by attaining popularity it enormously increases its own power and adds to the happiness of the subject; but in India popularity is peculiarly desirable, because an active sentiment of goodwill towards the supreme power alone can create in all classes that consciousness of a community of interests and sense of public duty by which, as I have said, they may be fused into one nation. But the Secretariat conceives the obligations of the Indian Government to be confined to the regular collection of revenue, the making of roads, the impartial administration of justice and the protection of the subject's life and property, that portion of government which it was in fact called into existence to supervise. But though it has usurped more than departmental authority, its political views have not been enlarged. It has no column in its statistical returns for the "Loyalty of the People", no index number for the "Popularity of Government." *

The form, then, in which I would put the popular indictment of the Secretariat is this: Government has neglected to cultivate the goodwill of the subjects and by elaborating the machinery of administration it has destroyed the agency by which that goodwill was partially secured in the old days of personal, I had almost said patriarchal, rule. A civilian 50 years ago had fewer returns to fill up and fewer reports to write, probably also fewer cases to decide; consequently he had more time to spare for making the acquaintance of the

* If the Secretariat had given a thought to the question of loyalty, this is how it would probably have dealt with it. The Secretariat measures the efficiency of all officers by a system of averages: it expects an *average* number of murders, rapes and thefts in a district. If the returns of crime are above the average the District Superintendent of Police is inefficient, since he has allowed crime to become rampant; if he makes a smaller return he is idle, for he has failed to detect crime. In the same way a Civil Surgeon must not perform less than an average number of major operations in the year, and in his report upon the management of the jail must not show more or less than an average number of punishments inflicted on the prisoners.

people. The Collector, too, generally remained for a long time in the same district and so acquired a personal ascendency over its leading men if, as was generally the case, he was intelligent and conscientious. Not only was the affection with which he was regarded imputed to the Government which he represented, but the Collector was able in friendly conversations (while perhaps he was shoot-ting or merely chatting to while away the tedium of camp life) to correct many misunderstandings and to dissipate the ill-will which some order of Government had created. Sleeman has left a record of many interesting conversations he had in the course of his rambles, and how often is one tempted in reading them to wish that a modern officer had time to talk to the people in the same way; the same complaints and the same misunderstandings prevail to-day, but an official would be thought grossly neglectful of his duties if he lingered to answer them as Sleeman did. It is true that the Government does recommend its officers to cultivate friendly relations with the people, but that recommendation must remain a dead letter as long as the routine of business engrosses all the working hours of the day. It is not in human nature, not in English human nature at least, to seek relaxation after a heavy day's work, by bandying the formalities of first acquaintance in a foreign tongue. As an agency of government, however, the Secretariat appears to set very small store upon personal influence; its ideal of the public services seems to be the machine-made watch, any wheel or spring of which can be transferred to another watch without inconvenience. How otherwise can we explain the changes which are continually made in the *personnel* of the administration, the constant transfer of a Collector from one district to another? Nowadays a collector hardly ever sees two successive crops harvested in the same district. In the one year 1893 each district in the North Western Provinces had to suffer from a change of Collector no less than four times. Is it conceivable that any one of these Collectors could have had the smallest personal influence over the people under his charge? The evil of these constant transfers is twofold; on the one hand, the officer's time and energy are wasted in getting up ever fresh facts and the peculiar details of ever new districts, and until he has mastered these he is practically in the hands of his subordinates, and Government does not get the benefit of his fullest efficiency. On the other hand it is impossible that the people should confide as much in a stranger as in a man they know. If they have known a Collector for some time they will submit their quarrels to him for arbitration, they will give him useful information about the state of the district and assist him in carrying out any project which he has at heart. The next Collector may be as good or better than his predecessor, but until the people are familiar with him he is, in all that concerns them, a worse officer. The harm which comes to the administration from this perpetual shifting of officers is now receiving tardy recognition, but matters would never have come to this pass had the Secretariat recognised the importance of attaching the people to the Government.

It is instructive to recall that our most successful Indian administrators, men like Henry Lawrence, Nicholson or Sir Henry Ramsay, whose names were a spell through half a province, were all soldiers. Not having been sophisticated in their early days by the Secretariat ideal, they approached the problem of government with fresher minds than our modern Civilians, and their regimental experience was not calculated to make them undervalue a spirit of willing loyalty in those under their command; the hearty coöperation of their subordinates, the *esprit de corps*, which they had learned to value in the regiment, they translated into the civil administration as loyalty to the Government.

The case then stands thus: public opinion upon politics is in India confined to a small fraction of the people, and these happen to be the classes over which the Government has most influence; so far, however, from using this influence to popularise the British Raj the Government in recent years has been losing the confidence of the people. This is due in the first place to that mistaken liberalism which exposes the Government to ceaseless attack and prevents it from being properly defended; and in the second place to the action of the Secretariat which has destroyed the personal ascendency of the local officer, an ascendency which in a fitful and irregular way was generally used to conciliate the people to the Government.

CHAPTER VII

THE COLLECTOR

WHEN considering the means by which loyalty to the Empress and her government may be inculcated, we are bound to recognise that we cannot rely solely upon the personal influence of officials. We have departed too far from the patriarchal system of government to make effective use of its methods; moreover, personal influence is so uncertain in its operation that it can at best be only an occasional ally and cannot be trusted to conduct the whole campaign. But I am not at all prepared to concede that the Government has been wise in abandoning its aid altogether. Although, therefore, I believe that the servants of the Empress should trust in the main to those broader agencies (the press and public education) which manufacture opinion wholesale, I would not abandon the attempt to modify it in retail, by the personal influence, that is, of her officers over individuals. The task would of course devolve upon the executive officers who come daily in contact with the people.

The unit of administration in India is the District, and it is therefore the head of the district, the official known in India as the Collector, who would be made responsible for giving effect to this policy. The average area of an Indian District is 3,875 square miles, containing an average population of 880,965 persons. At the head of each District, as the representative of Government, is the Collector, who, with his immediate assistants (Joint Magistrate, Assistant, Deputy-Collectors, Tahsildars, Naib Tahsildars and a numerous train of subordinate officers), and with the Superintendent of Police, the Civil Surgeon and the Excutive Engineer and his assistants, controls the executive machinery of administration. My proposal is that the Collector should be made responsible for the loyalty of his District, for the affection, that is, with which the inhabitants of the District regard the Empress and her Government, as definitely and precisely as he is responsible for the collection of the revenue, the condition of the roads and buildings, and the maintenance of the peace. His success in executing this policy would depend largely upon the personal influence of himself and his subordinates. The scope of one man's influence must always be limited, but the influence of all Government servants acting in one direction would be very far from unimportant in the society which formu lates public opinion in India. The Government of India would in the first place have to declare explicitly what political views it desired to encourage, and to insist that all its officers should hold these views as a condition of Government service. When the political opinions of Government were clearly defined, it would be the duty of the Collector to diffuse them by means of his subordinates among the people. Let us suppose, for instance, as an hypothetical illustration, that the Government decided to discourage the agitation for representative institutions, the political opinions, that is, of the National Congress. The Collector would then refuse to give any appointment to a son or relation of a notorious partisan of the Congress, and would strike members of that party off the Durbar list; he would explain to his native subordinates the reasons for which the Government disapproved of the proposal to introduce representation, and exhort them to use their influence in discountenancing these opinions. If any of his subordinates were convicted of expressing sympathy with Congress politics he would be dismissed from the service. A Deputy-Collector could as easily be tried by a departmental commission for expressing unconstitutional opinions as a military officer can be brought before a Court Martial for conduct unbecoming an officer and a gentleman.

It would of course only be by requiring the loyalty of the people to the Empress that the Government could escape the charge of disingenuousness, and could secure the honest support of its native subordinates; on this ground they would be prepared to think it a conscientious duty to popularise her administration. If it were known that such and such views were commended by the Empress and that these views and these alone were approved at headquarters, I believe that they would be adopted by the whole service and that the subordinate officials would vie with one another in spreading them among the people. But it is only by keeping constantly in the foreground the obligation to give effect to the wishes of the Empress that we can raise loyalty into the plane of ideas which would command the self-respecting adherence of the people; on this plea we should appeal to that sentiment of faithfulness to the salt (namak halali) which, as I have said, is so powerful among them. As for encouraging loyalty to our gracious selves, the English race, I cannot pretend to feel the smallest enthusiasm for such an object; I do not believe that it would be feasible or that Englishmen could play the farce out.

In order, however, to put the officials in a position to influence the opinions of the people it would be absolutely necessary to keep them for considerable periods in the same place; they could do nothing if they were shifted as constantly as at present from one end of the province to the other. I would suggest that the guiding principle of the Secretariat should be to keep an officer for the whole of his service within the area of one Division, that is, of six Districts. I do not propose to make the transfer of an officer from one Division to another impossible, for that would quickly cause great inequalities in promotion, but as a general rule it should be understood that an officer would have to serve the whole of his time within the limits of one Division. In this way he would become familiarly acquainted with all the big families with which he would ever have to come in contact, because most of the big houses hold land in two or three Districts; he would also be able to master thoroughly the dialect or *patois* of his Division in addition to that literary language which he is even now expected to acquire. Apart from the question of promotion, the objection which is likely to be urged against this proposal is that it would deprive the officer of the advantages of wide experience. I think that this is a sounding phrase which, in the particular case, corresponds with no real meaning. Within the limits of one province the conditions of one District are in all important respects the same as of another; the economic conditions are the same and the methods of government are the same; the differences consist chiefly of peculiarities of language and of new groups of individuals. Now it is no advantage to an administrator to have a smattering of half-a-dozen rustic dialects and an imperfect acquaintance with a large number of individuals whom he will never see again; what an English officer does want is a complete mastery of one dialect and the confidence, which springs from old association, of the particular individuals he has to govern.

If the Collector were entrusted with the duties for which I propose to make him responsible, he would have to be relieved of much of the work which he does at present, for he is already overworked. The manner in which that might be done is mainly a financial question, which would not come up for discussion until the Government of India accepted the principle of fostering loyalty to the Crown.

Were the Government to include popularity among the objects which it strove to attain, many more developments of this policy would suggest themselves than I can indicate here; one illustration must suffice. It has always seemed to me that one of the faults of the present system is that it has made life in modern India so oppressively dull and uneventful. This dulness almost amounts to a political evil, because it weighs most heavily upon the important class of the country gentlemen, the men, that is, who have an honourable social position and money at their disposal, but for whom the modern *régime* offers nothing to do. The answer of the hard-working English official is "Let them look after their estates." This is work which no doubt they might do both honourably and profitably if all they asked of life was the conscientious discharge of useful duties, but I never heard that the occupation of a land agent was particularly exhilarating; on the contrary, I observe that in England rich men generally pay somebody else to do it for them. In helping forward social and economic reforms India offers great scope to men of intellectual tastes and a high sense of public duty; but the majority of men are not intellectual nor deeply concerned for the public welfare. What such men ask of life is amusement occasionally diversified with spells of necessary work, and I do not know that in any but this tediously earnest age that would be thought an unreasonable demand. What the young squire in India with a good rent-roll would like would be to put his men in smart liveries and go to ruffle it in the capital of the province with his equals; that opportunity was offered him in the splendid court of Delhi, and is still open to a Muhamadan of the Deccan at the court of the Nizam; but in British India the life of a country gentleman is singularly barren and tedious; he has no society in his village but his relations and dependants; for miles around him there are none but peasants who, from the rise to set, sweat in the eye of Phœbus. Possibly he attempts to break away from this narrow life, and in turban of skyey grain and English boots journeys along sandy tracks to the headquarters of the District, the capital of his little world, and goes to call upon the English Collector, the greatest earthly potentate of whom he has any certain knowledge. He finds a busy man in riding-breeches, going about unattended, on a useful but certainly not showy pony. The Englishman speaks civilly to him in imperfect Hindustani; asks him how the crops are doing his way; then, after inquiring whether he wants anything in particular, informs him that he is very busy, and so dismisses him. Perhaps he then tries the Deputy-Collector in the hope that, as he is a native of India like himself, he may show him more consideration than the brusque Englishman; he goes with some confidence, for he is somebody in his own village, and he is gratified to learn that the Deputy-Collector knows all about him and can tell exactly how much revenue he pays to Government; but after a few minutes the Deputy-Collector, too, informs him that he must be off to court and that if he has any business he had better see him there. And in the evening? Well, in the evening he usually writes out his judgments, and just now he is very busy with a report the Collector is calling for. The young squire turns away and recognises that among these busy men there is no place for him. What then should he do in the town? He possibly wanders round the shops to buy European curiosities or presents for his people in the village, and as he passes down the street a few bedizened females salaam him from their balconies; they are the only diversion the capital of the district has to offer. Under our rule the natural leaders of Indian society have disappeared; the dignitaries of the state are the people who would naturally undertake the preparation of festivities and the organisation of a gala day in the East, but our dignitaries are all Englishmen and they take their relaxation at tennis or over a rubber of whist among themselves, and they generally make use of public holidays for shooting excursions. Were it not for the example of the Romans, who in these things are our masters still, I should hesitate in this workaday age to suggest that the Collector should occasionally organise a gaudy day in which rich and poor, English and Hindustani, should all have their part. Is it unbecoming the gravity of statesmen sometimes to give a thought to the pleasures of the people? The most successful Collector I have ever known organised a Gymkhana Club in the District, in which the landed gentry and the English officials used to ride. Our racing was not very high-class, but I always felt that our meetings were not without a political value; they formed a regularly recurring occasion for the native gentry to meet their English officials in a natural and unceremonious manner. If conversation was not spontaneous, there was racing or tent-pegging to watch, and the officials were not forced into an unnatural reserve by the suspicion that the native gentlemen had come to get some concession out of them; if a little pageantry had been added, the poor would have had their part in it as well. But it is useless to speculate upon such developments as long as the Secretariat limits the functions of government to the punctual despatch of executive business.

I contend that Government ought not to remain a neutral spectator of the present ferment of opinion which shows no tendency to arrive at any definite conclusion, but, having decided what political views tend most towards the creation of an Indian nationality, should throw the whole weight of its moral influence into that scale. I might well be asked why I confine myself to the moral influence of Government, as the logical development of my thesis would be that the Government should not only encourage certain views, but coerce others. My answer is that it might possibly be desirable if any government could be trusted to control opinion by force; but, as the late Sir James Stephen said, criminal law is a clumsy engine and its application to matters of opinion would certainly result in gross abuses which would do more harm than the ills it was intended to cure. However, the same danger does not lie in the use of persuasion, and the Government of India could afford to let its calumniators live if only it encouraged and rewarded those who loyally supported its policy.

CHAPTER VIII

THE PRESS IN INDIA

THE simplest division of the press in India is the newspapers that are owned and conducted by Englishmen, and the newspapers that are owned and conducted by natives of India. This last is again divided into two categories, the papers published in English, and the papers published in one or other vernacular. Broadly speaking, the papers that are conducted by Englishmen cater for the Anglo-Indian public and support the policy of the supremacy of the British race. This is by no means equivalent to supporting the Government through thick and thin; on the contrary, those papers which contend most jealously for peculiar privileges for Englishmen oftenest fall foul of the Government for what thay call its "weak concessions to native wishes"; but as all these papers are, as I said, written primarily for Englishmen, they contain much matter of no interest to the native public, such as news from Europe, and English society. The papers conducted by native Editors, on the other hand, whether in English or a vernacular language, exhibit greater diversity. Some of them are frankly the supporters of a political party,—for instance, a considerable proportion of those written in English (such as the "Amrita Bazar Patrika", the "Tribune" and the "Advocate") are staunch supporters of the Congress programme; but the vernacular press as a whole is less markedly political. In many of the papers politics are subordinate to the discussion of social or religious topics and items of personal news, which necessarily only command a limited public. There is proportionally a large number of ephemeral journals, with a very small circulation, which are started to give expression to the views of an individual or a clique, and as they are for the most part intended to advocate certain reforms within the community to which they appeal, or to give utterance to a certain body of ideas upon religious or social questions, their incursions into politics are uncertain and generally rare.

For my present purpose the essential thing to note is that among the papers which appeal directly to the native public, there is no important political journal which is a thorough-going partisan of the Government. Free institutions have disappointed our expectations in nothing more than in this. When we removed all restrictions on journalistic freedom we anticipated indeed that our government would be criticised and very often attacked, but we believed that we should have partisans who would vindicate our cause no less warmly, and that, as our Government is just and beneficent, our friends would preponderate over our opponents. But in practice we find that, though the agitators who wish to overthrow our supremacy are very conspicuous, those who do not profess to be dissatisfied with our rule are lukewarm and strangely indifferent to the calumnies which are heaped upon us. It is not true that the native press is unanimous in desiring to alter the constitution of the Indian Government; but thorough-going partisans, vigorous champions of our policy are not to be found outside a small circle of English editors, and thus the tone of the native press is either hostile or indifferent.

Surely this result should not really surprise us; it is the inevitable lot of despotisms; it is the price we must pay for autocracy. People all over the world start newspapers to promote certain interests or to push a hobby or to help forward certain ideas in the triumph of which they are concerned; but they do not found newspapers with the object of spreading abstract truth. To impart any spirit into journalistic warfare the matter in debate must be of a kind to be materially influenced by the writings in newspapers; it must be such that the decision lies in the hands of the public to whom the editor appeals, and whom he consequently strives to bring over to his way of thinking. The reason why most of our newspapers in England are such thorough-going partisans and impart such passion into the discussion of political questions is that their action is of great importance in determining the issue of the electoral battle, and the newspapers share as keenly as the party leaders in the elation of victory and the chagrin of defeat. But what can it profit a man to champion the cause of the Government of India? Only those educated in Europe believe that a despotism can be seriously shaken by newspaper criticism, and who is going to undertake all the vexation of a political campaign for a cause which neither needs, nor rewards his advocacy? A man would as soon fret himself in defending the precession of the equinox.

In another respect the native press has disappointed our expectations. Certain opinions obtain amongst the educated classes in India which bring in their train much dissatisfaction with the existing order. A very good answer could be made for the most part to these complaints, completely vindicating the Government, but no answer is given by the native press because there is no native editor with the knowledge or political insight to give it. The grievances complained of mostly refer to economic questions and might be illustrated by the following propositions, to which the bulk of the educated classes in India would give their assent: (1) India is getting poorer every year. (2) India to-day exports the necessaries of life and imports luxuries. (3) Famines have become more frequent in India since the establishment of English rule. (4) An export duty upon corn would be beneficial to India, but it is not imposed because it would make bread dearer in England.—In my opinion the first, third and last of these propositions are not true, and the second is a statement of an economic tendency which no government could control; but there is no editor in the vernacular press who possesses the statistical information necessary to make this clear to his readers.

Englishmen in India are apt to say that the malevolent tone in the native press is due to the large number of graduates turned out every year by our Colleges, who, unable to find employment in an overstocked market, betake themselves to seditious writing in the press. My own experience does not confirm the belief that the supply of graduates is greater than the demand at a very fair price, though possibly that price does not quite equal the extravagant expectations formed in student days. But even if it were proved that a large number of graduates fail to find lucrative employment, I should still reject the popular theory that they spend their time in writing seditious articles, because I am convinced that journalism in India does not pay. The "Hitavadi" (Bengal) wrote on the 12th January, 1898: "The statement that newspaper writers in this country take to abusing Government merely because they fail to make a living any other way is utterly unfounded. The idea of making a living by conducting a newspaper is an absolutely unpractical one in this country. Most newspapers in this country have to suffer pecuniary loss. Some manage with difficulty to make the two ends meet, while a few make some profit, but even these last can make no profit for years together if they have to figure as defendant in a defamation case. * An inquiry will satisfy the Government that almost every newspaper conductor in this country follows a different business as his living."

My own experience confirms this; I could mention many newspapers which are run at a loss, and I have had no personal experience of any which were a source of profit.

To whatever cause, however, the tone of the native press be attributed, this much is not generally disputed, that the regular perusal of the vernacular press by open-minded natives of India is likely to produce the belief that the Government is oppressive, unjust, and extortionate; and as men's views are mostly the result of what they constantly hear said around them, it surely argues no obstinate disloyalty on the part of the natives of India that they accept opinions and believe statements which they never hear contradicted.

While such forces have been at work to estrange the sympathies of the people from the Government, the executive have taken no pains to counteract the obvious tendency of a free press in India, or rather,

* The fact that the "Hitavadi" had just lost such a suit explains the rueful reference to defamation cases.

to speak truly, to secure to India the advantages that other nations derive from a free press. In order to secure these advantages our statesmen should have made provision that the case for the Government should be fully heard. So far is this from our actual practice that the real views of the officials are carefully kept from the public out of too faithful an obedience to the maxims of popular government.

When agitation for political privileges first began in India, and a certain section of the people attempted to justify their demand for change by disparaging the Government, it was the prevalent expectation that this section would be put down with a strong hand; but when it was discovered that the Government deferred to the opinion of these men, introduced some of the changes for which they agitated, and promoted the most conspicuous among them to posts of honour, a trouble and a doubt was cast upon the public mind; men began to ask themselves whether, owing to some strange unaccountableness in English nature, Government did not in reality approve of the Congress movement. The simple conception, natural to a country accustomed to despotic rule, that those who find fault with the Government are disloyal, was sophisticated, and men began to believe that the abuse of Government and the attempt to discredit it in the eyes of the people was, somehow or other, not inconsistent with loyalty. The distinction which Englishmen draw between the disapprobation of an alien Government and a disinclination to support the authority of that Government is sufficiently hard to perceive, but it was further obscured by the favour which Government showed to its most trenchant critics. A gentleman from Bengal has recently recorded how, in his youth, he delivered a speech in the presence of a former Viceroy: "I spoke," he says, "rank sedition, but I was received with compliments and indulgent smiles." Again, Mr. Tilak's methods of agitation were well known before he wrote the article in which he said that God did not give the Mlenchas (non-Hindus) the right to rule over the country. In a memorial signed by three Mahrattas and one Muhamadan, submitted to Lord Sandhurst in January 1897, Mr. Tilak's name is expressly given as being the chief organizer of a quasi-religious festival in which songs were specially composed, and circulated as leaflets; in these songs "references are made to the slaughter of cows, and appeals are made to the people to rebel as Shivaji did .... the poverty of the people which is represented in the songs as the direct result of the British government, the imposition of heavy taxes and the exchange compensation allowance, the topics of the day, are sung with zest under the cloak of religion." * And yet the Government of Bombay sanctioned the election of Mr. Tilak to the Governor's Council, one of the highest honours any Provincial Government has the power to bestow.

* Quoted by the "Pioneer" 8th July, 1897.

Thus old-fashioned people began to complain that Government made no distinction between its friends and its foes. Mr. Justice Strachey's famous summing up in the Tilak case came as a shock to this public which had ceased to believe that any abuse of the Government, short of direct incitement to rebellion, could be disloyal in the eyes of the law. I do not believe that an impartial jury of natives of India would have convicted Mr. Tilak. I do not mean to suggest that I differ from the verdict which was given; I have no doubt that it was good law, but, as the judge himself said, the law had been allowed to remain a dead letter and the native public had in consequence come to believe that it did not apply to journalistic writing.

This is a striking illustration of the way in which the *de facto* law modifies the opinions of the subjects upon questions of right and wrong. In the controversy which accompanied the amendment of the law relating to the press, it was made clear that the people of India in general had come to consider it unjust that the Government should put any check on the license of journalism. The genius of the people of India is essentially non-political, and it is not inherently probable that their views upon the proper limits of government interference would be of as much value as those of Englishmen. But it was a political error of the first magnitude to allow such a divergence to spring up between the conscience of the people and the law of the land, or what we now recognize ought to have been the law of the land. For that divergence the Government with its European canons of policy is solely responsible; there was nothing in the antecedents of India to predispose her to intemperate criticism of her rulers.

As I have just said, the arguments for the freedom of the press rest upon the assumption that there will be two sides to every controversy and that, if perfect freedom of expression be allowed, both sides will be represented in the press; upon this hypothesis it is perfectly reasonable to contend that in the course of controversy inaccuracies with regard to fact will be detected, sophisms will be exposed, and that on the whole the cause of truth will gain by free discussion. But the correct application of this maxim rests upon the original assumption that both sides are represented in the debate, and in order that both sides may be represented both must have an interest in the triumph of their respective views; now, as I pointed out above, the only persons who can feel a serious interest in defending the cause of Government is the Government itself or its officials; but they have been bound over to silence, and therefore in the present controversy on the merits of British rule the case for Government goes by default.

In this dilemma we may choose between two courses, viz., either silencing our critics, or making provision that the case for the Government be fairly stated. With regard to the first, it is hardly conceivable that Englishmen would ever enforce a press law sufficiently severe to put an end, not only to open attack, but also to indirect censure and to the suggestion of disapproval. A staple method of creating dissatisfaction with the present administration is to contrast it disadvantageously with a golden age of India, of which, to say the least, we have very slender historical evidence. Now, even in the teeth of a severe press law, a moderately intelligent editor could publish an historical essay on "India in the time of Asoka", which would excite invidious comparison with the state of India under the British. There must always be some people who have cause to be dissatisfied with the present, and nothing but a censorship of the press will prevent them from communicating their opinions to their fellows. My own sympathies are on the side of a free press, but I will here content myself with the argument that the attempt to silence our critics would be both unpopular and impracticable

We are thus driven to the second alternative, that is of making provision that the case for the Government should be fairly put before the people; and since, in the present condition of the vernacular press, there is no likelihood that a considerable number of editors will undertake the vindication of our rule, the task must be undertaken by the Government itself.

My proposal is that the Government should issue an official newspaper of its own, financed and edited by Government, and should also subsidise a certain number of journals which support its policy.

Such a proposal will of course horrify those who wish the Government in India to discharge only those functions to which its activity has been usefully confined in Europe, but it is the logical consequence of adopting the line of policy which I have suggested as suitable to the peculiar needs of India. The editor of the official organ would have to conduct a journalistic campaign on behalf of the Queen's administration. It would be his duty to show that the people are not worse but better off than formerly; that the importation of British capital has been a blessing to the country and does not, as is generally believed, drain it of its wealth; that the intention out of which unpopular measures (like the plague regulations) originated was kindly;—and above all a paper is needed which would circulate among the native public and would contradict and correct the inaccuracies and misrepresentations which too often pass unchallenged.

In order to make the Government organ succeed I believe that at first a comparatively large subsidy would be necessary, because at present vernacular journalism does not pay. Hardly any vernacular paper can afford to pay its contributors, and even so only a very small number succeed in defraying the expenses of publication. But to such a paper as I am contemplating, it would be necessary, in the first instance at least, to appoint an English editor with a salaried staff and to pay for contributions as well. An English editor would be required because I do not know where in native society a suitable man (who would be willing to take such a post) could be found, that is a man with the requisite statistical information and political insight and that general knowledge which is part of the stock-in-trade of an English editor. This English editor would have to work through a native staff because there is probably no Englishman in India with sufficient knowledge of any vernacular to attempt to write a leader in it. The Englishman would direct the policy of the paper and find the ideas; the native staff would throw these into suitable form.

My own experience of India has been confined to those parts in which Urdu (or Hindustani) is spoken, and I will describe what I conceive would be a suitable paper for the Urdu reading public. This Urdu paper would be published either at Delhi or Allahabad, once a week; in form it would be something like the London "Spectator" or "Saturday Review", save that the events of the week would be set forth with greater detail; it ought assuredly to contain information about the Queen, with such particulars of her life and of court news as would interest the people of India. Two or three articles would be devoted to the principal political events of the week, and for some time at least it would be necessary to publish a series of leaders upon economic subjects, so as to bring to the knowledge of the people some of the statistics which are familiar to all who have made even the slightest study of the economic history of India. But such austere reading would not be sufficient to fix the attention of the Urdu reading public; literary essays and articles upon social or personal questions would also be needed to lighten the paper; the Muhamadans, for instance, would have to be kept informed of the doings of the Nadvat ul Ulema, of the proposal to endow a Muhamadan University, and, once a year at least, of the business transacted at the Muhamadan Educational Conference; and the Hindus would similarly be kept informed of the progress of events in their community. The paper could also be made more attractive by signed articles from the most eminent Urdu writers; a poem by Dav, a literary criticism of Maulvi Altaf Hosain Hali, or a story of contemporary manners from the pen of Maulvi Nazir Ahmad of Delhi,—any one of which contributions would be sufficient to create a demand for the paper among readers of Urdu.

At the outset it would be desirable for the Government to have the paper taken in at every tahsil (administrative centre) in which Urdu was spoken, not so much to increase the circulation as to explain to the subordinate officials the policy of the Government at any given crisis; for, if the officials are to popularize the Government, it is necessary that they themselves should understand the reasons of the Government action.

I shall be told that official organs have been everywhere discredited, that the "Moniteur Officiel" has always been the laughing-stock of the public. This is true of European countries, but the experience of Europe has never proved a trustworthy guide in India. A newspaper conducted by Government is in Europe viewed with suspicion because people feel that Government is attempting in an underhand way to frustrate the will of the nation, even while it pretends to reflect it. But the Government of India does not pretend to govern according to the wishes of the people, and there is no national will to frustrate. In India it is the people who desire to know what the wishes of Government are, and I see no reason for believing that the people would view the statements in an official organ with distrust. The "Pioneer" (Allahabad) is understood to reflect official opinion, but it is not for that reason distrusted; on the contrary, I believe that much greater credence is placed by natives of India in the statement of fact in the "Pioneer" than in any vernacular paper. But the "Pioneer" cannot discharge the functions of a Government organ, because it is primarily written for Englishmen and contains very little matter of interest to a native of India; moreover, its tone (in its correspondence columns) is likely at times to wound the feelings of the people. I repeat that there is very little reason to fear that in India a Government organ would not be trusted; a much more real danger lies in the likelihood that a paper edited by an Englishman would get out of touch with the movements of thought in native society, and become as impotent for good or evil as a Blue Book.

I am not ignorant that certain tentative steps have been taken in this direction in the past by the Indian Government, but I think these ventures failed, not because they were officially countenanced, but because of their inherent unsuitableness to the public they were intended to address. One was a vernacular edition of an English paper, which was doomed to failure because it could not interest a native public; another attempt in this line was a subsidy to a paper conducted by a Muhamadan gentleman, who was indeed peculiarly capable of justifying the ways of Government to his own people, but who was viewed with intense suspicion because of his heretical opinions on religion.

I freely recognize that it would not be as easy to find an Englishman to edit the Government journal as to fill the post of Inspector General of Excise, or Director of Public Instruction. The first Civilian to hand would probably not be sufficiently familiar with the currents of thought in Indian society; but I am not willing to acknowledge that the English have so divorced themselves from the sympathies of the people that it would be impossible to find a suitable man. There is, however, one difficulty I must allude to, which is inherent in the scheme of a journal professing to represent the Government, and that is in regard to the many controversial topics in which Government, as such, is not interested; if these topics are wholly excluded, the paper will fail to excite interest; if they are discussed, there is a danger that Government would reap unnecessary unpopularity; the simplest solution seems to me that these subjects should be dealt with only in signed articles, for which the Editor, though in reality exercising a modifying control, should not appear responsible.

CHAPTER IX

EDUCATION

THE English value themselves not a little on the spread of enlightenment in India, but their zeal for the diffusion of learning has not proved sufficiently robust to digest the Calcutta B.A. That unfortunate graduate comes beneath the lash of every whipster who airs his views on Indian politics. The plethoric Major, whom he staggers with unfamiliar learning, says he is the curse of the country; the weedy Under Secretary, for whom he tabulates averages in the alien air of Simla, accuses him of spreading sedition; the Editor of the "Pioneer" satirizes his manners, and his little vanity in patent leather shoes, and the London papers call him the Frankenstein (*quantum mutatus ab illo* of Mary Wolstonecraft) which the Indian Government has raised. The last nine years of my life in India have been spent in the manufacture of the B.A., and I cannot find it in my heart to call him any of these hard names. My estimate of his importance in the scheme of creation may differ from his own, (a view which I have never thought it necessary to conceal from him,) but that he is in almost all important respects greatly superior to the majority of the generation whom he succeeds, cannot be seriously denied by anyone familiar with native society. He comes a long way short of an ideal standard, no doubt; but what reasonableness was there in ever measuring him by such a standard? It is a legitimate and sufficient ground for congratulation that he possesses a much greater sense of public duty than his parents; that in the administration of justice for which they usually took bribes, his hands are clean; and that upon him depend the reforms in religious belief and social usage which are troubling the hitherto still waters of Indian society. These are solid merits which it is ungenerous not to recognize because our fastidious taste kecks at some crudeness in his manners, and the licentiousness of his political oratory.

Indeed, if we consider what English education in India really connotes, we are astonished that with means so imperfect it has already achieved so much. Education, as it is understood by the Government is purely intellectual. It is contended that in a country of so many religious beliefs, in which each religion prescribes a peculiar ethical code of its own, a neutral Government could not undertake religious or moral instruction, and accordingly the work in an Indian College is severely confined to disciplining the intellect. When the

Indian student has matriculated in a University, he leaves his village home and establishes himself in some large city like Lucknow or Calcutta, and is enrolled in a college. He is necessarily entrusted with comparatively large sums of money; he lives where and how he likes, and renders no account to anyone of the way he spends his time. After attending classes for four or five hours a day, at which an Englishman, who perhaps does not even know his name, expounds certain text-books, he returns to his lonely lodgings and dubious acquaintances in the bazaar; it is nobody's place to ask him how he spends the remaining 19 or 20 hours of the day, and he spends them in such company as may take the fancy of a boy of eighteen. After four years of this life, his education is said to be completed, although it is extremely improbable that in that time he has come into contact with a single man of elevated character. When it was pointed out some years ago that this education was weak on the moral side, the Government suggested to the University that a remedy might be found by prescribing a moral text-book. So might a French Ministre d'Instruction Publique attempt to modify the domestic habits of the Quartier Latin by prescribing the study of Telemaque, did he not know too well how Murger would delight to construe it for the edification of Mimi in their draughty lodgings.

The most obvious comment that will suggest

itself to any experienced schoolmaster, is that this system of education does not include the two most powerful agencies for moulding the character, viz., the personal ascendency of the teacher and the corporate life of the school or college in which boys administer a code of conduct upon themselves.

With regard to the first, an English principal or Professor has no chance of acquiring any personal influence over his pupils, because he has no natural opportunities of meeting them except in class; if he wishes to see them, he must make the occasions himself or explore the malodorous kennels of the bazaar to find their lodgings, where his unfamiliar presence would create dismay. Admiration for a superior intellect and a character more elevated than his own, is the beginning of every boy's moral improvement and lies at the root of the whole conception of education; it is the secret of every good mother's training of her child, and of Dr. Arnold's influence over a whole generation of Englishmen. The Pundits and Maulvis of old days lived in familiar intercourse with their pupils, and consequently exerted on them an influence beyond all comparison greater than we can pretend to. Our modern system in India sets the master and the pupil apart, and the consequence is that the generation which has been instructed by Englishmen neither reverences its teachers nor follows in their footsteps.

The second charge that might be brought against

University education in India is that the youths are dispersed about a large city instead of being collected within the college walls, and thus no opportunity is given for that corporate opinion or code of honour to come into existence, which boys enforce upon each other with so much rigour. If any body of young men be collected within four walls and made to live together, they will, even though no provision be made for their direct edification, come in time to an agreement upon principles of conduct, and will enforce the strictest obedience to this self-composed canon of behaviour; in the words of Newman: "they will administer a code of conduct and they will furnish principles of thought and action. They will give birth to living teaching, which in course of time will take the form of a self-perpetuating tradition, or a *genius loci* as it is sometimes called, which haunts the home where it has been born, and which imbues and forms, more or less, and one by one, every individual who is successively brought under its shadow." I do not contend that without proper guidance the standard of behaviour evolved in an Indian College would necessarily have been a desirable one; if the unnatural divorce between the master and pupil had been maintained, it might have been vehemently hostile to the English and to the rule of the Empress; but I do believe that it would have been an enlargement of the mind, that the principles so acquired would have had more force to influence conduct than any pedagogic homily, that they would not be so soon forgotten in after life, and that they would have formed the nucleus or foundation of a school of opinion which would have leavened the whole of the educated class. And though a practical schoolmaster will recognize that he cannot exactly drill the thoughts and wishes of young men like a squad of soldiers, bidding them go this way and not that, yet he can by excluding certain influences and encouraging others, greatly modify the opinions of his scholars, and at length produce a tone in his institution closely corresponding with his wishes. My own experience is that the student in India is far more amenable than the English schoolboy, or irreverent Undergrad, to the influence of his teacher. The tradition yet lingers of loving reverence on one side and a parental authority *(non sine ferula)* on the other.

For these reasons I believe that a remedy for many of the evils from which English education is suffering, would be found in the addition of boarding-houses to the existing colleges, in insisting on residence in them as a condition of enrolment, and in entrusting the management of them to the Principal with an increased staff. This is a reform which I advocate in the interest of education; but if it were adopted it would greatly facilitate the task of enlisting the sympathies of the educated classes on the side of the Queen's administration, and of making them, what they should always have been, her most loyal subjects. The Englishmen who composed the staff of these residential colleges would be in daily contact with their pupils and have many natural and unforced opportunities of mixing in their lives; clubs and societies are sure to spring into existence, in which the professors can put off their donnish solemnity and appear with more amiable attributes. A student who had felt in his youth a strong attachment and reverence for an individual Englishman, is not likely to be without some friendly feeling for the English in after life; such friendships would certainly abate something of the ferocity with which the educated classes now denounce the English and all their works in India. In such a college a professor has many opportunities of talking politics in an informal way, and it is improbable that the students who come to ask his advice upon their domestic or pecuniary troubles, and consult him on the choice of a career, will be absolutely indifferent to his opinion in matters upon which he is much better informed than they. It is an absurd mistake to suppose that the Indian student is perversely and obstinately disloyal; he is perfectly capable of understanding correct reasoning and ready to be convinced by it, if the facts and arguments are only put before him; but an appreciation of the excellence of the present administration does not come by nature, and there is no reference to the subject in any of the text-books he has hitherto been taught, which is the only educational agency recognized by Government. Is it then surprising that he holds views which he never hears disputed, and believes facts which he never hears challenged? In the debating societies which the students are sure to found, an English professor would have an opportunity of setting forth his views at length, and he would indeed be unfortunate in his endowments if he could not succeed in dismissing the case against the Government as it is usually presented. But whether in private conversation or public debate, the presence of an Englishman, who was not vehemently prejudiced, would introduce an element of sane reasoning which would lift the discussion of politics into a higher level. There is no error to which the boy politician of the East is more prone than a rash generalization, which, whether true or false, has not been arrived at by any approved method of induction; a temperate demand for the facts which bear out these sweeping assertions would cool many a perfervid orator and not be disrelished by the audience.

The modification of their political views would only be one aspect of the influence which the English staff would exercise upon all the opinions of their pupils; but such an influence is necessarily uncertain and irregular in its action, depending as it does upon the personal character of the Principal or professor and his interest in politics. The Principal ought, however, to recognize that it is a part of his duty to make sure that the prevailing tone in his college, regarding politics, is loyal to the Queen's administration. Each man must realize this object in the manner that appears best to himself. I have found that good results follow from calling senior students together and discussing with them in a friendly and unofficial manner some of the leading questions of the day, especially the reasons for measures, such as the recent Plague Regulations, which have excited great popular ontcry. I found the students eager to come, and not at all backward in stating their views; and I never felt the least temptation to disguise my real opinions, even when they did not coincide with the policy of the Government. I had no occasion to regret these incursions into politics, and I afterwards discovered that if I had not succeeded in modifying the opinions of all who came there, I had at least brought over a considerable number to my way of thinking, and that in consequence a division of opinion was formed, and after the meetings came to an end the discussion was maintained in the college upon the lines that I had originally indicated.

There is one political opinion which I believe that the Principal ought to impart in his official capacity, and regarding which he has as much right to overrule private judgment as upon a question of morals. The Principal should teach his pupils that loyalty to the Empress of India is a civic duty. So far from being repugnant to the feelings of the parents, this action of the Principal would, I believe, receive their conscientious approval. The people of India hold that obedience to the Sovereign is a moral obligation; the Hindus believe that a ruler is an incarnation of the Gods, (a *præsens numen*) who ought to be obeyed like the Gods; and the Muhamadans (however much Christian controversialists may malign them) consider it a religious obligation to obey a ruler even of a different faith, who allows them the free exercise of their religion.

Such methods as I have here suggested for securing the loyalty of the educated classes are matters of the internal discipline of the college, and have no reference to their studies for the University Examinations. The work of the lecture rooms ought not, I think, to be subordinated to any political aims; but there is one branch of learning much neglected in India which would profoundly modify the disapproval with which the British rule is regarded; that study is the economic history of India. Now the economic history of India, in the last 100 or 150 years, stands upon its own pretensions; it is worthy on its own merits to find a place in a liberal education; it would form an admirable exercise in the application of the abstract theory of economics which is at present taught in India, and would impart to the student a vast body of knowledge quarried from Government Reports and Blue Books. The diffusion of this knowledge in native society would be of immense political value. No political opinion is so wide-spread as that India is getting poorer and poorer every year, and this belief is a constant source of ill-will and disaffection; it forms the burden of every complaint against the British rule, and is shared with melancholy conviction by those who take no part in political agitation. I believe that this view would be dissipated by a patient and scientific investigation of the facts; but those who hold the contrary opinion can hardly object to its study. The material for a sound history would be found in the diaries of old travellers who visited India in the last century and the beginning of this, in the journals of those soldiers of fortune who sold their swords to the Mahratta, the Sikh or the Nizam; in the reports of early Collectors, in the forgotten Revenue Reporter, the publications of the Statistical Bureau, the Census Reports, and the evidence given before the great Commissions. The weighty report of the great Famine Commission of 1880 alone contains more economic wisdom than has yet been brought together to support the contention that India is getting poorer. In addition to this, much information might be got by hunting for indigenous records, such, for instance, as the account books of the corn-dealers and money-lenders. This enormous mass of facts requires to be digested and co-ordinated before it can be presented to the student, but I personally have very little doubt what answer it would give to a patient and conscientious inquirer.

The educational policy which would, I believe, win over the educated classes to loyalty may be briefly summarised as follows: the Universities should prescribe the study of the economic history of India; the Principal of each residential college should impress upon his students that loyalty to the Empress is a civic duty, and he and his staff should live on terms of friendly intercourse with their pupils and so wean them from the belief that Englishmen necessarily either despise or dislike the natives of India; they must mould individually, and one by one, each generation of scholars, until at last a tradition takes root in our Colleges that the abuse of the existing administration is neither patriotism nor good sense.

NOTE ON EDUCATION IN INDIA

I

FOR those who are interested in education in India I add a few remarks of a more technical nature. I do not think it advisable that residential colleges should be directly controlled by the Government; I think that better results would follow if such colleges with their endowments were handed over to a body of native Trustees or Governors, chosen to represent a special community or religious sect. Thus, to illustrate my meaning by a practical example, I should like to see the Government College at Benares handed over either to a local committee chosen from among the Hindus of Benares, or to a body of Trustees selected from the Hindu community in the North West Provinces and Behar. This Committee or Board of Governors would lay down the broad outlines of the policy to be pursued in the internal management of the college in accordance with their own religious and ethical convictions; they would in other words make the existing college a denominational college for Hindus; they would direct the Principal to enforce the observances of the Hindu religion as a matter of college discipline, and to prohibit the use of those things which the Brahminical law forbids. I believe that morality so taught would have more power to influence conduct than any eclectic system of ethics which Government would be willing to enforce, because, in India at least, an ethical system is likely to be accepted in exact proportion as it has the sanction of religion, and a system which has not that sanction will not command more than a languid obedience. The task of administering internal discipline would be greatly simplified if the Principal had but to secure the observation of one religious law. A Principal can make strict rules and secure obedience to them if he is legislating for a homogeneous body; but he would fail in exacting obedience to them if the rules could only be applied to certain individuals in that body. The Puritanical austerity of Islam, for instance, would forbid Muhamadan lads to dance, sing, drink wine, or play upon a musical instrument, to all of which the Muhamadan boy is as inclined by nature as any other boy. Now these habits or recreations in moderation are not forbidden to the Christian or Sikh or certain sects of Hindus; but no practical schoolmaster will feel any confidence that the Muhamadan boys are not drinking or singing with their schoolfellows of another creed, if he is obliged to indulge some of his pupils in these practices. A Principal who had one definite ethical and religious code to administer would not only find it easy to enforce it, but would also receive the support of the parents, who as matters now stand are generally inclined from political animosity to take the side of the recalcitrant pupil. It is this consciousness that they have not got the parent at their backs which makes the Principals of Government and Missionary Colleges apprehensive and timid in enforcing discipline; they spare the rod because the one is afraid of raising a political outcry, and the other of offending a public which at best only tolerates him. But if the details of internal discipline had been sanctioned by a body which commanded the respect of the community, the parent himself would approve of a salutary vigour in the administration. What Hindu of Eastern India will deny the right of the Pandits of Benares to regulate his son's conduct? and what site so appropriate for a great Hindu

College as the sacred city of the Ganges?* Can any Englishman contend that the moral teaching of the Brahminical Law is not a hundred times more elevated than the practice of the bazaars of Lucknow? The Muhamadan lads who inhabit Benares would have to go elsewhere, to a purely Muhamadan institution, for their education. Let them argue how Auranzeb would have wished his people to act by lifting up their eyes to the mosque of the great iconoclast which stands above the city, withdrawn from the contact of the abominations of the heathen.

The Hindus of course would need several such denominational colleges; for the North West Provinces alone three or four would only be barely sufficient; one Khalsa College at Amritsar would perhaps satisfy the Sikhs; the Muhamadans are already attempting to found a university of their own, and the Parsis would find it no difficult matter to build a college for themselves in Bombay. For some time to come these colleges would all require pecuniary assistance from Government, but I would limit the direct participation of Government in education to the control of one college in each province, which should teach only the B.A. and M.A. classes.

* Subscriptions are actually being collected in order to found a Central Hindu College at Benares upon the lines here indicated, but Government has not yet been able to give the movement official encouragement.

Even after retiring from the direct control of education, Government would have no difficulty in getting the denominational colleges to adopt its educational policy and insisting that the students should be brought up as loyal citizens. There are many colleges already in existence which are not managed directly by Government, and my proposal is but the extension of a system which has been found to work well. Almost all these colleges receive a grant-in-aid from Government, and in an even greater number the governing bodies are much influenced by the wishes of Government. The Government, while giving them great latitude in religion and secular education, may reasonably make its grant-in-aid conditional upon their turning out loyal citizens: if any college proved recalcitrant and chose rather to forego the grant-in-aid than to adopt the official policy, Government could reduce it to immediate submission by refusing to admit the students of that college into its service; no college in India could keep open a week after the publication of such a rule; before the week was over every student would have deserted its class rooms.

II

It will have been observed that I have confined my remarks to collegiate education with special reference indeed to the B.A. classes. I recognise of course that the great majority of what are known as the English-educated never reach the B. A. classes; a large number never read further than the university Entrance or matriculation examination; of those that push forward more than half are swept away in the Intermediate or First Arts Examination; it is only a dwindled band of survivors which struggles on to the degree. But none the less it is the college students and especially the B.A.'s and rarer M.A.'s which set the tone of the schools, not the schools which influence the colleges. This is because the schools of India are not institutions which, like our great public schools, stand upon their own pretensions, with sentiments and traditions of their own; they rather stand to the colleges in the position of preparatory schools, and they copy the tone of the higher institution; many colleges indeed have schools attached to them and the two stand to each other exactly in the relation of Upper and Lower School. The Indian schoolboy therefore moulds himself upon the B.A. of the college. This tendency is further assisted by the masters of the schools, who are mostly graduates of one or other university and bring with them and impart to their pupils the opinions and prejudices they acquired at college. Any attempt to modify the opinions of the educated classes must therefore be directed against the colleges; the idea of bringing about any considerable change in them by means of instruction imparted in the schools, is as futile as attempting to purify the Thames at London by regulating the sewage of Oxford. I am not here combating an imaginary misconception; the Government of India is actually attempting to eradicate the disaffection of the educated classes in this very way; and I am the rather led to call attention to the question because it shows how the logic of events is compelling the Government against its own professions to interfere in the formation of political opinion and to abandon its policy of non-interference. Recently, that is to say since the disturbances in Poona and the trial of Mr. Tilak, the Government has prescribed in schools the study of a book called "The Citizen of India"; it is a good little book containing a great deal of accurate information in a small space, but it is professedly a panegyric of the present administration and deals with a great deal of controversial matter in exactly the opposite sense to Mr. Dadabhai Naoroji and the National Congress. How the schoolmasters in Government service are to teach this book and obey the regulation of Government which forbids them to take part in politics, I leave to their consciences and the Director of Public Instruction. My question is solely, will it effect the object for which it was prescribed? The book is written for young boys, and the author cannot therefore give the evidence upon which he bases his conclusions. Will the boys then accept these opinions upon his authority?

That depends entirely upon the commentary with which the master chooses to embroider it. The author says that the Governments of former days spent nothing on canals, roads, or public works; they were unable to protect the villages (contrasted with the capital) from foreign enemies and left them to their fate; in times of famine and pestilence they took no action to save the lives and properties of the suffering masses; all of which facts and much more are often categorically denied in the native press. The boys may accept this as historically accurate if their master confirms it; but, as he is generally a graduate from one of our universities, he will probably not. He will, I expect, say that it is palpably untrue, that the writer is an Englishman who knows nothing about India, and will proceed to enlarge on the prejudice with which the book is written, illustrating this thesis from such passages as that in which the author, in his anxiety to do the best for his client, has actually suggested that the reason why Government does not allow volunteering is that the distances in India are very great and the caste system would greatly reduce the usefulness of volunteers. Everybody knows that the real reason, to put it crudely, is that the Government dares not trust the people so far. But even supposing that the schoolboys were convinced, would these convictions (the convictions of a boy of 14 or 16) stand against the public opinion of the college, against the views held by those older and more important than himself, with whom he has now to mix? The opinions he will hold in manhood depend not upon the ideas he imbibed at school, but upon the surroundings in which he is to pass the next half dozen years of his life. The Government of India has tinkered with the question, enough perhaps to create irritation, but not to effect a cure.

CHAPTER X

THE PART OF THE EMPRESS IN THE ADMINISTRATION OF INDIA

AT the outset I have assumed that our intention is so to govern India that she may one day be able to govern herself, and I contended that that day will not arrive until India becomes a nation, or at least until in her different provinces a national sentiment arises conterminous with definite territorial limits. I have argued that we cannot bring such a sentiment of nationality into being except by encouraging the various communities that inhabit India to unite in supporting one central authority, be that central authority common to all India, or distinct for each several province. I have tried to show that if loyalty is based upon devotion to the person of the Empress, it will be readily yielded by the people of India, and that it is our duty to encourage and foster that loyalty by all means in our power, because *salus reipublicæ suprema lex*, and that statesmen are therefore justified in employing all the resources of the commonwealth to create the conditions without which the very existence of the state is precarious. I have tried to show that in her present stage of development it has been a mistake to apply to India those principles of Government which have been formulated for states co-extensive with nationality, and which affirm that it is not expedient that the resources of the commonwealth should be employed to guide and influence public opinion upon politics. I contend that the reverse is true in India. I have stated that I am opposed to the coercion of opinion, not because it would be ineffectual, but because I am confident that no Government could be trusted to use such tremendous powers judiciously; and that I believe that it is expedient that the Government should publicly avow certain political opinions, and should require its officers to hold those opinions as a condition of service, and to spread them among the people; and that honours and emoluments should be exclusively reserved for those who support the official policy. I have further urged that wide publicity should be given to the political views of Government by means of official newspapers in the vernacular; and lastly, that these views should be instilled in the young in all those higher educational institutions which receive a grant-in-aid from the state.

But there is one condition upon which the success of this policy depends, and on this I must insist at the risk of tiresome iteration; that condition is that we must ask for the loyalty of the people of India, not for the English race, but for the Empress of India; the supremacy of the Empress is the only principle of Empire which they can recognize without loss of self-respect, and it is the only one which we can in decency put forward.

Now I do not think it would be impossible to persuade the people of England to sanction this policy, for it is in harmony with some aspects of that imperial sentiment which has grown so much in their esteem of recent years. But the different aspects of what is sometimes called Imperialism require to be carefully discriminated. In those portions of the Empire which are mainly peopled by the British race and which Seely aptly called Greater Britain, Imperialism is but the recognition of the unity of that great people, whatever lands are its home, and of their determination to keep undivided the magnificent inheritance which their ancestors carved out of the new world; it is a large patriotism founded upon pride of race, and, as long as it is confined to Greater Britain, it is as unequivocal a good as patriotism has always been recognized to be. But in countries such as India or Egypt, in which the bulk of the inhabitants is not English, and in which Englishmen are only administrators and governors, it is not desirable that this pride of race should be publicly expressed; in such countries it becomes, instead of patriotism, merely an expression of the conqueror's arrogance and of the humiliation of the native population. The proper form for the imperial sentiment to take in our dependencies is pride in and devotion to one great Queen, who rules indeed over many lands, but who is equally the mistress of her white and brown and black people. In Australia, Imperialism may find expression in some British variation on "Yankee Doodle", but the imperial anthem for India is "God save the Queen". Greater Britain might prosper and hold together even if our crowned republic were by a process of constitutional evolution to get rid of every trace of its monarchical origin; but, for India and the dependencies, the only principle of cohesion is to be found in common obedience to an individual monarch.

As, then, the Queen of England is already *de jure* Empress of India, what we mainly need is to bring that fact home to the people; to keep as far as possible out of sight that unlovable machine called the Government of India, and to get the people to realize that the Empress is the source of all authority in India. Napoleon III seems to me to have appreciated very justly the importance of bringing before the public the sovereign's part in government. In an interesting article in the "Revue des deux Mondes" of 15 February, 1898, Mons. Emil Ollivier says of him: "Peu de souverains ont été aussi impersonnels. Aucun de ses actes n'a été dicté par un interêt égoïste ou de famille, il a toujours recherché le bien public et n'a jamais songé qu'à rendre son peuple grand et prospère. Toute-fois, il ne supportait pas de voir d'autres se parer d'une résolution qui, même conseillée par eux, n'existait que par sa volonté. Prêt à supporter la responsabilité du mal auquel il ne s'était pas opposé, il n'admettait pas qu'on lui dérobât le mérite du bien qu'il avait permis. En ce sens, il était personnel, ombrageux, jaloux de son pouvoir." It is rather a matter of words than of the exercise of new powers, but it is none the less expedient that our statesmen in India should accustom themselves to attribute a larger share of administration than they are now in the habit of doing to the beneficent wishes of the Empress.

It is never wise to divest a government of all the attributes that appeal to the imagination of the people, for loyalty is an emotion, not a proposition which is intellectually perceived. If what I am about to suggest may seem to some fanciful, and unlikely to add to the material happiness of the people, I would answer them that our Government in India has failed, in so far as it has failed, just because it has sought nothing but a dry administrative perfection, and that what it needs for its completion is just the warmth and colour which surround the person and the court of a splendid monarch, which do not indeed either fill the belly or lighten the load of a single coolie, but which dazzle the imagination of rich and poor alike, and invest the power, which is else only dreaded, with personal and therefore lovable attributes.

The Empress's undoubted prerogative, of appointing whomsoever she chooses to posts in her administration, is in India a most valuable power, and if Her Majesty were to exercise it more frequently, she would be held in India to be discharging the most important function of Government. The people of India, as I have said before, are not keenly interested in the application of political doctrines, and consequently they do not trouble themselves much about legislation, which forms the centre of political life in democratic countries; but they are very keenly interested in the distribution of patronage and are quick to detect any new departure in the making of appointments. Now they very naturally suspect their present rulers of partiality in filling the posts to which they have, or hope to have, a claim; they expect that Englishmen will give the preference to an Englishman in making their selection for an honourable and lucrative post; and they complain that in practice they are not able to rise to the positions which the regulations of the service justify them in expecting. A monarch would be less likely to be suspected of this partiality, and for such an opinion there is, I think, a very sound reason. Monarchy is a form of government especially suitable to an extensive empire, just because the interest of the monarch is not generally identical with the interest of a dominant caste. On the contrary, the monarch will frequently desire to diminish the irksome privileges of his nobles, and will look to the subject race for means to counterbalance the excessive influence of the few. As Mirabeau foresaw and Napoleon demonstrated, the cause of absolute monarchy gains by the abolition of a privileged class. I do not of course mean to suggest that the English Royal family would ever desire absolute power, but I do think that they would naturally and inevitably be inclined to bestow honours with a liberal hand upon their native subjects, and would strenuously resist all attempts to make the Indian services a jealous monopoly. There is, I think, another reason why the people of India would have reason to congratulate themselves if the Empress used her prerogative of appointment more freely. In filling a post, the sovereign is likely to consider the political effect of the appointment, whereas the members of a service generally confine their attention to the fitness of an individual to discharge the duties required of him. We cannot of course expect, or even desire, that the Empress should personally make appointments in India to any but a very few posts, and those of great eminence and dignity—the subordinate appointments must be made, as at present, by the senior members of the service;—but these few and eminent posts are just those of which the political importance is greatest. The political effect of appointing a native of India to one very exalted post is vastly greater than that of putting hundreds of them in subordinate positions. It may well be that the aggregate salaries of the inferior officers are much larger than the salary attached to one highly paid post, but the imagination of the people is kindled at the sight of one of their own race in such a position of honour and confidence. Within my own experience in the North Western Provinces I have seen that the appointment of Mr. Justice Syed Mahmud to be Puisne Judge of the Allahabad High Court, gave the Muhamadans of Upper India incomparably greater satisfaction than they ever derived from the contemplation of numerous Muhamadan Deputy-Collectors, Tahsildars and Kanungos. Now it is, I contend, a part of statesmanship to consider the satisfaction which an appointment may give to the native population, and this satisfaction may fairly be weighed against the superior efficiency of another claimant; and it would from time to time be wise to risk some loss of efficiency for the sake of the popularity which would accrue to the Government. I believe that the Empress, being so far removed above the details of administration, would recognize the political expediency of appointing a native of India from time to time to a position of great dignity; whereas I do not think that the Indian Civil Service would ever take anything into consideration but the respective efficiency of different candidates, and this principle of selection must, for many years to come, result in the exclusive nomination of Englishmen. If, however, it were the Empress's pleasure to appoint a native of India to be Lieutenant-Governor of one of the provinces, and if, for her sake, the English in India acquiesced loyally in the appointment, I cannot conceive any inconvenience to the administration which it would not be worth while to undergo for the sake of the popularity which would accrue to the Empress of India.

Let me reassure those Englishmen who would be dismayed by such a suggestion. For many years to come the proportion of natives to Europeans in the highest branches of the service, to which alone the Empress could give her attention, must remain very small; Englishmen of the requisite character and education may be found in hundreds where natives could only be picked out by ones and twos. From a political point of view, however, the numerical proportion is not very important; what is important is that the people should feel that their own kith and kin are as much trusted and as much honoured by the Empress as her own countrymen, and a very few posts are sufficient to create this impression, if they are really among the most exalted the Crown has to bestow. The Hindus extol the justice and generosity of the Moghul Emperors because they appointed Hindus to be governors of provinces and commanders of armies, but such appointments must in reality have been very rare; the great bulk of the officials seem to have been Muhamadan; of the courtiers whom Sir Thomas Roe or Bernier saw in attendance upon the Great Moghul, very few bear Hindu names.

The appointment of a native of India to a very prominent position, hitherto held by an Englishman, would undoubtedly create a very serious social difficulty; and as, for six months of the year at least, the headquarters of Government are in the hill stations, which are more and more becoming English towns where the native population counts for very little socially, this difficulty is more likely to increase than diminish in the future. I cannot pretend to think that the disinclination of Englishmen to admit the natives of the soil into their society, does not present a very grave, perhaps the gravest, problem connected with British rule in India. If anything I could say would contribute in the smallest possible degree to a satisfactory solution of the difficulty, I should esteem it of more worth than anything I have yet written. But what can be said on this subject which it were not much better to have left unsaid? I can only hope that the English might possibly accept from the Queen an innovation which no Viceroy could persuade them to tolerate.

The intervention of the Empress could with less difficulty wipe away another reproach to our rule. The natives of India have just cause of complaint against us in that we do not admit them to posts of military command; the youngest subaltern from

England ranks above a veteran native officer, who perhaps fought for the Queen at Sabraon or Chillianwala, and no native of India can ever hope to rise in the British army above what is in fact the rank of a non-commissioned officer. This is the most solid ground the people have for saying that they are not, in practice, treated on an equality with Englishmen. There are enormous difficulties in the way of making any change, and I have never heard of any feasible plan by which natives of India could be admitted into the regular army. If, as has been suggested, an Indian Sandhurst were established, from which officers were selected by open competition, I doubt whether one man would pass who was fit to set a squadron in the field. The boys who succeed best in competitive examinations in India are generally wanting in all the characteristics needful to a soldier, and our gallant native officers very rarely have the qualities required in the higher positions of military command. Every other suggestion that has from time to time been made for admitting natives of India into the regular army, bristles with difficulties; but the same objections cannot be made to their admission to a special and exclusive corps. I venture to think that the Empress herself might devise a partial solution of the problem, by raising a corps of Imperial Guards, to be officered by the aristocracy of India. Such a corps would be small and exclusive, and would establish no inconvenient precedents for the regular army. It would perhaps not consist of more than three regiments, chosen from those races which had most distinguished themselves by bravery in the field and loyalty to the Crown; a regiment of Sikhs, a regiment of Rajputs and a regiment of Muhamadans would not only fulfil these conditions, but also represent the aristocracy of India. It would be expedient to give both officers and men higher pay than is the rule in the Indian army, for in Asia it is generally felt that the liberality of the Sovereign is concerned in giving wealth as well as honour to those immediately attendant on his person. To the commissioned ranks, however, none ought to be admitted who did not belong to the wealthy landed aristocracy, and it might confidently be predicted that the officers of the Imperial Guard would be far more prone to lavish expenditure than to an unbecoming parsimony. The proudest house in India would covet a cadetship in such a corps; and as it would be important to reserve the honour to only the very noblest families, one or two should be selected in each district by the Collector for the privilege of sending up one of their sons to a competitive examination to be held in India; the successful candidates would then proceed to Sandhurst, where a further weeding might be found expedient before they passed out. When the regiments were first formed it would be necessary to put an English officer in command to imprint a becoming military tone on the young corps, and to establish a proper tradition of smartness and efficiency; but when the first English commandant's term had expired, the regiments should be left to the entire charge of their native officers.

The Imperial Guards would of course have the special privilege of guarding the person of the sovereign when in India, and what monarch could desire a more splendid escort than a corps picked for their magnificent physique from the martial races in India, and clad in the resplendent uniforms becoming an Indian Imperial Guard? Such a body should not, however, be kept solely for processional purposes; they should be worked hard at camps of exercise and given liberal opportunities of seeing service, that the officers might have a chance of showing whether or no the natural leaders of Indian society have in them the stuff of which rulers of men are made, as the rank and file certainly possess the courage to follow wherever they are led.

I trust that I shall not be thought fantastical if I suggest that a palace should be got ready in India for the Empress, against the possibility of her coming; it is desirable that she should let her Indian subjects know that she does not look upon India as a foreign land in which she fears to set her foot, but as an integral part of her Empire in which, did health permit, she might occasionally take up her residence, and in which she would be as much at home as in any province over which she holds sway. As a matter of fact, her royal fortresses of Delhi and Agra are given over to desolation; unsightly barracks for a meagre garrison have been built upon the ruins of palaces, and ammunition boots grind upon the marble pavements which were smoothed for the tender feet of princesses. Clear the waste places inside the royal ramparts in which English soldiers now play football, sweep away the barracks and the canteen, and in their place build a palace worthy of the greatest sovereign that ever ruled in India. As yet the only architectural monuments of the Empress's reign have been canals and bridges and railroads; it surely would not be extravagant to raise one building which should appeal to the unsophisticated sentiment of her subjects, and should connect her name with the places in which their sovereigns have always resided. Even the dullest imagination would be kindled at the sight of the royal standard floating over the majestic gateway of Akbar's fort in Agra; of the British horse guards in their polished cuirasses, lining the gloomy court of guard; and of the royal cavalcade, attended by a gorgeous retinue of Indian noblemen, emerging from beneath the venerable archway.

Unfortunately the great age of the Queen forbids us to hope that she will ever come to India. Had it been possible, we can fancy with what a tumult of emotion her coming would have been greeted, and how her presence would dissipate the clouds which just now darken the outlook in India. We can fancy how she would hold her royal court at Delhi or Agra, and summon into her presence her feudatory princes, the governors of her provinces, the leaders of her armies and the great noblemen of her realm, and unfold her mind to them with queenly directness: "I have done more for my people in India than any sovereign who ever sat upon this throne. I have not spent my revenues upon jewels or palaces, but upon railways and roads, upon hospitals for your sick and upon canals to water your crops; I have given you peace within my borders, and I have fed you when you were hungry. You have repaid me with grumbling and discontent. You have reviled my ministers and slandered my Government. I am displeased with this ungrateful fault-finding. I desire that it should henceforth cease, and I have directed my servants to honour and promote those only among you who are heartily loyal to me and my administration."

THE END.